4586

The Centrality of Preaching
in the
Total Task of the Ministry

The Centrality of Preaching
in the
Total Task
of the
Ministry

by
John Killinger

WORD BOOKS, PUBLISHER
WACO, TEXAS—LONDON, ENGLAND

Library of Congress Catalog Number: 69-12817

Grateful acknowledgement is made to Alfred A. Knopf, Incorporated for permission to quote "Anecdote of the Jar" from The Collected Poems of Wallace Stevens.

For my teachers,

GEORGE A. BUTTRICK and PAUL E. SCHERER,

who, more than any other great preachers
of this or other ages,
inspired in me the high confidence in preaching
which is expressed in this book

CONTENTS

INTRODUCTION

"Praedicatio verbi dei est verbum dei," said Luther—"The preaching of the word of God *is* the Word of God."

This was the high view of preaching with which the Great Reformer emerged from the contest with Rome—not the one with which he entered. It was a derivative of experience, which is significant, which says, in fact, that it is no mere theological slogan but an absolute truth of life to be observed empirically by anyone who consistently preaches the word of God or faithfully beholds such preaching. Somehow, in a mystery, the declaring of that hard and sometimes ambiguous word merges with, becomes, even *is* that Word itself, so that no one can find the end of one and the beginning of the other, that seamless seam where they first entered into one another and lost their separate identities, God becoming incarnate again and what was carnal, fleshly, becoming somehow God, or Word of God, active in our midst, probing, destroying, cleansing, saving.

It was no idolatry of preaching that Luther held, no thought that in and of itself it deserved a place in men's esteem, but rather a notion that preaching is the substanceless intersection, the bodiless point, where paths divine and human cross, leaving wonder and merriment in their wake. God is still all in all—all, that is, except for the alienated fragment, the disaffected body, the broken-loose humanity he tries again to reabsorb in fellow-ship, which attempt, when it is successful, is a miracle of sorts, absorption without absorption and freedom *into* God. And preaching is that point without weight or distance where he makes himself known and felt—and heard—most notably.

It is with a similar conviction of the importance of preaching, not just in Luther's day but in ours as well, that I undertake the development of the theme of this book.

I know it is not a popular theme. The word is out, among pastors and church leaders as well as among seminary students, that preaching doesn't work any more, that the moving finger has passed over it and is now pointing us to inner-city reclama-tion, discussion groups, world-awareness studies, renewal of liturgy, and other kinds of "modern" ministry. Most of the men entering seminary today come with very little use for the busi-ness of preaching, intent instead upon hermeneutical "secrets" or theological subtleties or ethical styles which they regard as the be-all and end-all of theological education, capable of wafting them away once and for all from the ordinary parish, which they inwardly fear the way they fear the penitentiary or the insane asylum.

One need not wonder at this. There has indeed been a failure of preaching in our day. There are not many pulpits in this country (which, incidentally, is better off than most) where congregations may count on hearing an authentic word, a true word, a life-saving word, Sunday by Sunday. I live in a com-munity that is almost over-churched, literally, where thousands of acres of church property increase the tax burden of the entire citizenry, and a surfeit of church morality, or pseudo-morality, seems to stifle the very air we breathe. And I know from months of anxious searching and sermon-testing that there are at best half a dozen preachers, out of nearly a thousand in the city, who may be depended upon to have produced a message which is not, at worst, an insult to the mean intelligence of the congrega-tion, and, at best, an affront to the best human imaginings in the contemporary era.

Sometimes one begins to wonder, in a time of anti-plays and anti-novels, whether there ought not to be a corresponding anti-sermon, a sermon denying the formal structure and approach of the sermon as we have known it now these many centuries, if for no other reason than to accomplish what the anti-plays and anti-novels are out to accomplish, namely, the ultimate and long overdue demolition of hollow forms and dry usages that are no longer filled and lubricated by imaginative and exciting content. It is so evident that the sermons set before most congregations today (and it was only rarely ever very different) are like those unpalatable pastries costing their hosts or hostesses little bother and less thoughtfulness. Their preparers know little of what Joseph Sittler has called "the anguish of preaching," which is as indispensable to true preaching as it is to poetry and music and art that are true.

All of this is to say that it is grossly unfair to blame preaching for the debacle it has experienced in our day. It is not preaching that has failed, but preachers, preachers and churches. Churches too must bear a part in the responsibility for not having insisted on better in their pulpits, for not having helped to shape the preaching, or at least to have said, as one British monarch is reported to have demanded of a clergyman who was fulminating before him, "Either talk sense or come down." There is no reason to suppose that preaching, when it is really preaching, has had its day and is done for. The fact that the word "preachy" or "preachery" has come to have a pejorative effect as a modifier only indicts the kind of sermonizing that has so frequently passed for preaching; it leaves untouched the profound work and mysterious nature of true preaching, preaching at its best, preaching as transaction between God and man. We must discriminate between the two kinds of preaching, and remember that it is always the second kind, preaching as supreme poetry, that is intended for recommendation by this book to the centermost place in a man's whole ministry.

This book is written with the consciousness that many ministers today need to be pointed to the center again, and reminded that, for all the siren lures of dilettantism, they can never satisfy either their callings or themselves by being all periphery, all circumference, touching on many things, but without an anchoring place or a pivot providing reality and substance to what is at the edges, where things so easily become illusory. The tragedy of so many young men leaving seminary is that, lacking a proper conception of preaching and ministry, they quickly become unhappy with their roles as ministers. They begin to feel that their relationship to society is a merely tangential one, when what they really want is to affect society deeply, operating directly at its core. They watch the bankers and manufacturers and politicians in their congregations and dream of being like them, of wielding power and living in pomp, of making decisions without always consulting this or that committee (so innocent are they of the world of business), of being men of action in a real world where action is really possible (so little they know of the real world). And they seem never to have become aware of why it is that these men they so admire come to church on Sunday, why they continue to come even in the face of the church's failure toward them, because they want some word of hope for the misery of their existences, some ordering factor that will clear their minds and hearts and dispel the insanity always threatening at the door, some gospel to exorcize the demons mocking them in their forty-dollar shoes and twenty-foot Cadillacs.

Over and over, the story is the same. A young man goes to seminary and winds up in a church. He tries to enlighten the congregation according to the tag-ends of theological and biblical esoterica he has picked up in the course of his formal training—though he is hardly into his parish a month before he begins to be frightened and confused at how limited and frequently inapplicable they seem to him. Convinced that he is hired to be some kind of medicine-man, he feels invariably called upon to introduce his professional mumbo-jumbo into the conversation, whatever its course or subject. This is particularly true in matters touching the Bible. Disturbed by the easy familiarity some of his parishioners, particularly older women, exhibit about the biblical literature, he soon resorts to impressing people with his fussiness over textual transmission and matters of translation. His favorite phrase, or at least his oft-repeated one, is, "In the original manuscripts"—as though he had the least notion of what was in the original manuscripts, or would even recognize one if he came face to face with it. The congregation sees him as a nice boy who will probably mature into a very decent sort of minister (although by then he will have been called to a larger parish), and is prepared to be casually tolerant of his greenness and occasional bumptiousness while he is proving himself to them and the world (and most of all to himself).

But he is in a hurry to do big things. He can't help it, bless him; he thinks he is as mature as he will ever be, or else he suspects maturity of carrying inside it the seeds of its own failure, such as timidity and fear of insecurity. He is anxious to turn the world upside down before he is thirty, never wondering what he would do with it if he did manage such an unusual feat, never understanding that it is childhood's dream to do so precisely because it is childhood's reaction to insecurity. After a few months, he is nearly out of his mind because he has not even achieved the reformation of the Sunday school roll, much less of the world. He begins to burn with slow insatiable anger at the congregation sitting there before him clothed in its tolerant little smiles and half-listening to his self-important little homilies, while the other half of its mind, the bigger half, is thinking how pleasant it is to be in the sanctuary, with the flowers and the organ music and the stained glass, composing itself for the dreary onslaught of the world outside, the world at home, the world on Monday morning. One day, having decided that he is taking his salary under false pretenses, and that the congregation has no intention of letting him fulfill himself on it the way he inwardly yearns to, he resigns and declares his mission ended, his intention now of taking other work. Maybe he even hefts all the blame onto the situation of the modern church, and, calling up the assistant editor of some true confession magazine he has covertly bought and read, he tries in a last instance of piracy to turn a fast dollar out of the failure of his ministry by committing his disgruntlements to print.

This history is sad but true, and many a man will recognize some shadow of his own ego in it, perhaps many years afterwards. Some will even admire the boy for having deliberately chosen the exit, instead of having endured the slow chiseling death they have felt because they wanted out but couldn't stand the guff from friends and loved ones, or couldn't overvault the economic pressures, or simply couldn't find another job.

It is for these, these lifeless ministers condemned to live and thus exhaust their fates, and for the young, who need to be told how it is before they arrive at their first parish, that these words are written; and also, perhaps, for some who know the truth of what is said but have forgotten, have allowed to elude them in the manifold pressures of parish life and administration the matchless insight that might have made magic of all their work, might have saved their souls—and their weekly sermons—with wonder and amazement.

One word of warning: reading a book like this is no real substitute for the actual experience of preaching. There is always the danger that the comfortable minister, the one who knows he can get by a while longer with things as they are, will get his kicks from reading about what he ought to be doing instead of from doing it. It is one of life's many varieties of voyeurism. The earnest reader, who does not approach his daily study merely as a chore to be got out of the way, will lay this book down the moment he gets an idea of what he should be preaching or what he should be doing in his ministry, and will return to it only when he is too tired to be about first things or when his inspiration has evaporated and he hopes to find more.

ANECDOTE OF THE JAR

I placed a jar in Tennessee,
And round it was, upon a hill.
It made the slovenly wilderness
Surround that hill.

The wilderness rose up to it,
And sprawled around, no longer wild.
The jar was round upon the ground
And tall and of a port in air.

It took dominion everywhere.
The jar was gray and bare.
It did not give of bird or bush,
Like nothing else in Tennessee.
                    —Wallace Stevens

1

The Centrality of Preaching

In the castle of William the Conqueror that adorns the high hill at the center of Lincolnshire in England, there is a most remarkable little chapel, small but deep, with the pews tiered rather steeply in a semicircle, somewhat in the manner of an ancient Greek theater. The pews are actually narrow single stalls, with the backs rising up and over the persons occupying them like cowls or panoplies; and, as the seats in them are mere sloping pedestals, to be leaned against more than sat upon, they give one the uneasy feeling of being in some kind of medieval torture device like the famous "little-ease." The pulpit, mounted by a keenly inclined set of stairs, almost a ladder, is set about halfway up the wall opposite the pews; and, the pews rising precipitously as I have described them, it is but a very brief distance from the pulpit to the pew in any part of the room. The worshiper, sitting or leaning with a sense of extreme tentativeness in his box, can see nothing in the chapel but the pulpit. Try as he will, he cannot see another worshiper like himself, either beside him or below him or above him. His gaze is irrevocably determined: it must be upon the preacher!

17

Whoever the architect was who designed the little chapel, though long since passed into oblivion, he had for his day, when men were still erecting Gothic cathedrals and elaborating the ones already standing, a most remarkable eye for the centrality of preaching in the ongoing life of the church and its members, and he wished to make it impossible for others to miss what he saw. For a man in medieval times, he was possessed of an unusually modern vision. He was a Reformer before the days of the Reformation, with an exceptionally high opinion of the mystery of preaching.

But standing in that chapel recently, I was moved to consider not only how different it is from other places of worship built in the same era—from Lincoln Cathedral, for example, which stands only a little more than throwing distance from the castle with the chapel—but how utterly foreign it is to most churches today. There are few places in our own time where preaching stands so unmistakably at the center of Christian thought and experience. The pulpit is no more centripetal-making, no more range-finding, no more the focus in most churches today than it was in the forgotten age when that clever little chapel was devised. If anything, churches are more muddleheaded than they have ever been, more confused and uncentered and unconvinced of where their centers, their foci, their jewel-studded navel buttons really lie. They tend to be like that liberally witless congregation in Peter de Vries' novel *The Mackerel Plaza,* with its split-level building and split-level mind, with a pulpit (indeed a whole sanctuary) nearly lost in the shuffle to have a convertible activities room and a neuropsychiatric clinic all on the same modern diminutive building lot. Preaching to them, real preaching, preaching that becomes the Word of God, is only a part of the racial memory, a dim thing from the vague past whose only possible use in the present is to twit the minister with his general inability to reproduce it.

Men today are generally suspicious of any kind of prolonged verbalization, especially when it proceeds out of the mouths of either preachers or politicians. They have been so bombarded by words, so deluged by them, that they have found it impossible any longer to believe them. They are not ignorant, stuttering cavemen like their ancestors, nor even untutored, credulous children like their more immediate fathers. They are the most literate, informed, and competent audience that any speaker ever had, and therefore they are the most difficult, the most incredulous, and the most impatient.

It is hardly a wonder that one man wrote to Bishop Robinson after the publication of *Honest to God* and said, "I have a deep inner desire to return to church, which I find I can satisfy by attending church service abroad where I can understand nothing of the message, yet can be reminded by the environment and by the deeply reverent attitudes of the worshipers, as well as by the magnificent music and the religious pictures, of the intention behind the ritual, and of the deep religious experiences I used to feel as a boy."[1] He had to worship, but could not stand the words; therefore he found satisfaction in a pantomime, a service where he understood no words.

One suspects that this is the way it is with many a church-goer today. Tired of clichés, burned out on the worn-weary rhetoric of a pulpit desperate for something to say when it has lost its primary vision, he plods through the motions of being a churchman—church-school teacher, vestryman, trustee, even lay-man *extraordinaire*—and secretly, without even admitting it to himself or confessing it to his wife-confessor, deplores and detests the time given to, surrendered for, *lost* on preaching and prayers. It is a weary, dreary, humdrum way he travels, and he would, if he could, retrace it to the junction where he took the wrong turn, where he was a reasonably happy, carefree pagan (and maybe therefore more like a real Christian), and go the other way. But he can't do that, so he keeps on going the way he is going, and feeling guiltier and guiltier and half hearing ever more distantly the word that might free him, might release him from his guilt.

---

[1] *The Honest to God Debate,* ed. D. L. Edwards (London: S. C. M. Press, 1963), p. 53.

Marshall McLuhan, in that crazy, provocative book called *Understanding Media,* raised a real issue, because it is on the underside of all our minds today, when he said that words, as media for any kind of message, are dead. (He is consistent, even though he is a writer, for he told a reporter once that the mistake all the critics of his books have made is that they suppose him to be saying something!) Suppose it is true, that we have passed out of the Gutenberg era, the era of print and words and logic, into the era of technology and television, when life is imploded, resonant to total impact, and words no longer make a dint apart from sound and color and movement and all the rest that constitutes what, for want of a more explicit word, we call our context. Judaism and Christianity are religions of the Word; they have always flourished, in periods of renewal, linguistically. Preaching, by McLuhan's definition, is a "hot" medium, highly defined, nonparticipational, granting a minimum of freedom to the audience. How can it be expected to coexist with television, which is a cool medium with low definition and high participation, and with the liberal mentality produced by television? The implication, of course, is that it cannot.

So the average church and the average minister, profoundly aware of a malaise that affects them and the whole of civilization, continue to go 'round the mulberry bush, loudly decrying the apostasy of the times but speaking in whispers of the fainting and disaffection they experience beneath the hollow masks of their own composure. They talk a great deal about the erosion of faith and the erosion of preaching and the erosion of culture and the erosion of everything else on earth they think they understand, but without one good guess as to what may be done to throw up dikes or barricades to stop the floods that cause the eroding. The preacher complains that the people do not really want him to preach, that they prefer instead for him to be a factotum, a manager of paperclips and memoranda, a kind of avuncular sexton to the whole community, a soothsayer who soothes instead of saying sooth, a fetish for a sort of religion-in-general, a Father Murphy figure in a business suit; and the people complain that the minister is not really a preacher, that he spends too much time trying to be a man-about-town, religion's gigolo at the civic clubs, and that they wish he would hew to his study at least part of the time and stop setting before them so often those insufferably stale breakfast cereals he is pleased to call sermons.

The truth is, McLuhan and all the prophets of the twentieth century to the contrary, that people are not tired of preaching but of non-preaching, of the badly garbled, anachronistic, irrelevant drivel that has in so many places passed for preaching because there was no real preaching to measure it against. I have not forgotten the expressive face of one man, a medical doctor, who was speaking of the rich experiences he was having under the ministry of a certain preacher who had recently become his pastor. "Somehow I had never come to expect," he said, "that I should hear a good sermon every time I went to church, or even every other time. It just never occurred to me that it should be the normal, Sunday-by-Sunday experience. Now I don't know how I could bear to go back to the way it used to be." It is the same with most people; until they have had the good fortune to sit under a really good preacher (and, sad to say, most people never do), they don't know to expect any better; they merely assume that things are bad all over.

I remember another man's having said of his minister, "I cannot stand to hear him preach, he tortures me so. It is as though he looks through a window in my heart and knows exactly what I am like, exactly what I feel, exactly what I am thinking. He senses feelings in me I have not even realized I felt, so that they strike me with the force of sudden recognition. I cannot stand it. But neither can I stand not to hear him. When I miss a week, as I sometimes must, I feel as if some unbearable heaviness, like a fog or a mist, had settled on me for the week."

The use of words has not really gone out of fashion; it is just that so much more is demanded of them today. In an age so critically attuned to the stimuli of technopolis, when men's sensory apparatus is literally under bombardment from all directions, they must not only bear much closer scrutiny than before, but must, unprecedentedly, create their own milieu. The preacher can no longer get into the pulpit and speak the private language-signals of his particular school of theology (there might be much more reason to speak of *prisons* of theology instead of schools) or even of his particular religious tradition. If he is in any kind of community at all, and not just some sociological backwater, he cannot count, as his predecessor of a generation or two ago could, on facing a congregation which has as a characteristic any kind of true homogeneity. He faces the some phenomenon that playwright John Osborne has said the writer for the theater must confront today, where the only thing uniting the audience is "the climate of disassociation in which it tries to live out its baffled lives."[2] His words therefore must reveal a genuine intimacy with the brokenness of the times, an intimacy which inevitably humbles theology and philosophy, and must stand somehow by themselves, without benefit of former preaching tradition, in evoking the images and directions which give promise and hope to life. The clichés of a rural, frontier theology are an insult to the intelligence of his present cosmopolitan hearers: if they bear those clichés at all (and many will not, as the exodus from churches has proven) it is not gladly, but out of the hugest tolerance imaginable.

Identifying authentic preaching is not difficult when one hears it; describing it is quite another matter. Like most professors of homiletics, I have often pondered how one might best delineate it for students, so that it is finally evoked in their sermonizing and they can recognize it, thrill to it, and, hopefully, become dissatisfied with anything less. But it is not a simple thing. There is no foolproof recipe, no guaranteed method, no step-by-step account. "The preacher is born, not made," wrote a friend to Paul Scherer when she heard he was leaving his pulpit at Holy Trinity Church to teach homiletics at Union Seminary. And there are times when one feels that this is almost true, that

---

[2] "John Osborne on the Thesis Business and the Seekers after the Bare Approximate," *The Times,* October 14, 1967, p. 20.

unless a man has got the gift inside of him there is nothing that can be done with him or for him or to him to turn him into what one ardently wishes he were.

Perhaps one approach to the meaning of true preaching may be made by an analogy to art. I do not mean the kind of art that is bound for the museum (although good sermons may be legitimately printed between hard covers for basically the same reasons that some paintings and sculpture make it into the museums); I have always feared the art-for-art's-sake philosophy in any area of human endeavor, and especially in the matter of preaching. I allude instead to the experience of the artist who *discovers* something as he paints, or the poet who discovers something as he composes. There is a kind of mystery involved in the process. The artist does not know at the outset where he will end up. He begins with his technique and with an idea, but the idea is not inert; it grows, conceals itself, reveals itself, dodges, feints, comes on strongly; before long it absorbs the artist, controls him, uses him. The more practiced an artist he is, the more this is true. In the end, he knows that he did not really make the work of art; he has been the instrumentation by which it has come into being, a kind of midwife to its birthing; it possesses an integrity of its own; it has fulfilled itself, that is, has filled out the lines of its own promise and potentiality; and the artist is enriched for having served it, for having spent himself in its realization.

Imagine now: sermons arrived at in this manner, given a preacher whose mind is well disciplined in Christian thought and secular technique, are actually pieces of revelation—just as good poems and paintings and sonatas are. Only, as the preacher lives constantly closer to the dreaded center of life's meaning ("I am crucified with Christ," said one), it is to be expected that the revelation in his work will plummet faster and surer and more breathtakingly to the heart of any matter (would it were true!). What he does will be continually characterized by what Matthew Arnold called "high seriousness," by that thoughtful, noble movement, that clear-eyed and elegant carriage which first prompted the phrase "the royalty of the pulpit."

I have seen a few preachers who fit the characterization I am sketching—maybe ten or twelve out of the hundreds I know. But it is enough to assure me that I am not talking mere theory, mere gobbledygook, mere nonsense. The making of the sermon is actually a moment of revelation, a trip into the holy mountains, for them, and the delivery of the sermon is such a moment for their congregations. Their preaching galvanizes men—upends them, probes them, haunts them, follows them into their most remote hiding places and smokes them out, drives them out coughing and sputtering and crying into the open light of new grace and new freedom and new love. The withered are made whole, the lame leap for joy, the dumb find articulation, the confused discover direction, the harried find resources for slowing down—in short, there is an apocalypticism about such preaching, an immediate grasp of what is yet distant and still to come, a taste of what is promised.

The human community needs this kind of preaching, indeed is perishing for want of it. The crisis of human identity, compounded out of war and technology and urbanization and wealth and poverty and boredom and overstimulation and excess and deprivation (all the crazy-quilt contradictions that exist juxtaposed or even superimposed on one another), has never been more acute, more demanding, more absorbing than it is right now. Ionesco has caught the flavor of it in his dramas—of men crowded off the stage by inanimate objects, by furniture and mushrooms and eggs and, in one play, by a corpse that won't stop growing, that just keeps swelling and swelling and extending itself all over the house; of men who cannot communicate any longer, not even in simple, unrhetorical prose, not even in everyday, casual conversation, but who speak senseless *non sequiturs* and answer banal remarks with totally irrelevant replies; of men who, lacking now the confidence of being human, of even knowing what human is, begin to lay eggs or to bark like dogs or to grow horns and become rhinoceroses, abandoning even the pretense of being persons.

Martin Esslin wrote a book about this kind of drama and

called it *The Theatre of the Absurd*, and the name stuck. But the reason absurd theater has had a hearing, the reason Ionesco has had one play running in Paris for over ten years and Jean Genet has become an off-Broadway sensation in New York and Edward Albee and Harold Pinter have become world-celebrated for their crazy but cunningly cruel portraits of life, is that for many people, even the finely accoutered gentlelady and the nattily attired businessman in the church pew on Sunday morning, this is the way it is, this is the way life is today. On the outside it is polished and orderly, like the fadeless nylon supersmooth plastic medicated and antiseptic expedited and wall-to-wall carpeted world we move around in; but on the inside it is broken, confused, hellish, anguished, lying in pieces, and crying its eyes out. Did ever a preacher have an audience with more of a star-sighting, depth-anchoring, stack-poling, axis-making need than this one? Name him.

And this is precisely what the Word is about—it is about creation called out of primeval chaos, about Tiamat slain by a fiat, about a ragtag sloven and servile people summoned out of slavery, about a government achieved in a wilderness, about a Kingdom coming at night, about *Christ,* and the nameless fear that still keeps men in chaos and bondage and night and death until they have heard, really heard with the ten thousand ears of their souls, the news, the announcement, the *word* of his coming, his being here, his significance. Who was it, Bailey of Newcomb, who spent three hours every night after working as a clerk from seven in the morning till six in the afternoon, writing the word Christ on little slips of paper, which the following day he would leave in men's mailboxes, buggies and milk bottles, hoping they would wing their way into little crevices of the mind and stay there until some moment made auspicious by grief or anxiety or even unexplained joy? However crude the method ("I know the Bible says we should be fools for Christ," said an exasperated John Mackay to the students at Princeton one day, "but, boys, it didn't say 'damn fools'!"), the notion was correct. It *is* an ordering word, a life-centering word, a home-finding word. It *does* plant hope smack in the middle of the desert of despair.

I cannot count the number of times that I myself have gone to church so smothered by despair and dejection that I hardly hoped for an inkling of a word to penetrate the fog I was in—the dense, choking, strangling, death-dealing smog of a soul forgetful of life and love and devotion—only to have some minister (maybe even a fumbling, bumbling, incompetent one) say something (maybe even marginally, a hundred thought-miles from the point he was trying to make) that pierced the mist like a solar ray and brought me back surely and soundly to the glory of existence all around me. And if it has happened to me I know it has happened to all manner of men, for there are none that are harder to reach with the spoken word than the speaker of words, the preacher on a busman's holiday.

Who knows, when he preaches, how many thirsty tongues cry out before him, eager for the Word that is a fountain in desert places, a stream whipping over dry rocks? Who knows when he will say precisely the thing that is needed to rejuvenate some soul honeycombed with the fissures and lines of age and care? Who knows when he will be the instrumentation for this man's discovery of strength, or that one's renewal of hope? Who can guess when he will be the bearer of some word that becomes a flag of health and promise in the low-lying mists of another person's despair and bitterness, a standard-bearing word for rallying the man's life and putting him back on the way to joy and love again?

If we only remembered this, how much more eagerly we would set about the composition of our sermons! The drudgery would be gone. We would rejoice at paying whatever price is necessary to the accomplishment of our one great aim, to set a life-saving, soul-ordering word loose in the midst of a congregation of human beings, and then to see it work!

But there is another side to the matter too, an inside side, so to speak, and that is that the more a man works at his preaching, so that it becomes a dependable word in this briar patch of words we inhabit, the more orderly his own life and ministry tend to become. The more he applies himself to this demanding task, this rushing-waiting, listening-speaking, anguishing-thrilling, plaintalking-poetizing, burning-freezing pinpoint in his navel of navels; the more he will discover a sense of orderliness in his ministries of paperclips and memoranda, telephone calls and afternoon teas; the more he will know who he is and what his game is and what the rules of the game are. He will gradually cease to think of himself as a religious cowboy wearing a red-white-and-blue "I like God" button on his chest and trying to keep his greased feet in the stirrups of a bucking, jolting piece of ecclesiastical machinery that nobody to his knowledge has stayed on very long. He may even begin to relish his pulpit chores as the most exciting part of a generally stimulating vocation, and to awaken ahead of the rest of the household on Monday morning in order to get down to his cubbyhole in the basement and to the apple crates he uses for a desk and enter that magic womb of creation where he and his preaching are reconstituted week by week.

There is nothing like preaching, when it is imaginatively conceived and faithfully executed, to bring order and meaning into a man's entire ministry. A man must have a center. He cannot be all circumference. Somewhere, somehow, things must come together. And the burden to preach, to make a sermon, to speak a word, is such a place.

It is with preaching as it is with the work of art in the little poem by Wallace Stevens which stands at the front of this book; that is, preaching becomes a point of reference from which patterns are put upon life. It should be noted that Stevens took pains to emphasize that the item set upon the hill in Tennessee was not, as we might have expected, an urn or a vase, but a jar. In other words, we are not dealing in his poem with something esoteric or sophisticated, but with something common. This is most appropriate in a disquisition on preaching, for we are not talking about the unusual, filigree sort of preaching found occasionally in avant-garde churches and university chapels, with which we are of course delighted, but about the good solid meat-and-potatoes everyday fare in preaching which should be expected in every village or county seat church. When the jar is put on the hill, the wilderness, the sprawling crawling chaos of trees and undergrowth, is suddenly no longer a wilderness; it has an imposed center, and the chaos "wheels to" around it. There is now a point of reference, a stackpole, an axis. Order has been introduced into disorder.

This is the claim I make for a good theology of preaching—that it introduces order into the chaos of a man's ministry. He is lost in the thicket and tangle of crisscrossing paths and dense undergrowth. A dozen major responsibilities tug at his sleeve, this way and that. Administrator, educator, counselor, prophet, pastor, social worker, maybe custodian, secretary, mimeographer, plumber, carpenter, and husband and parent on the side—he is expected to be many things, indeed even wants to be. But there are definite limits to his time and energy and psychical composure. He would like to be all things to all men, but there are times when he feels the need of saying, "This one thing I do." And the one thing claiming precedence over all the others, demanding to stand at the center, because it has been the distinctive, necessary task of the ministry in every age, is the matter of proclamation. Nothing else will substitute for it. Its priority is absolute. It alone is capable of bringing to heel the multitudinous and variegated duties which yip and yap at the minister's coattail like mutts of hell wherever he goes.

Let me be as candid as possible, and address the reverend clergy directly. As a preacher in an age when preaching is widely regarded as the bogus currency of a bankrupt ministry, the best thing you can do, for yourself and your ministry, is to set the business of preaching at the very center of your life and work, and give it first claim on your time and energy. This may appear to fly in the face of what has come to pass for the natural order of things, but it is the only way. Invariably it is the men who have done this who are successful in the multiple areas of their ministries, and the men who have not who are frustrated and discouraged and fearful that the house is falling in on them.

The mere physical act of reserving certain hours of the day or certain days of the week for the preparation of yourself and your message will begin to impose order on your schedule. With a kind of silent eloquence, this will help to assure you that at least *you* know what you're about. It will remind you that beyond anything else you may happen to be, you are the bearer of a Word men need to hear, of a Word they cannot do without in their lives, and that you must consecrate yourself to that high office.

You cannot hope to lead people along the inner and outer contours of the faith unless you have thus fenced off the hours for your own exploration of them. You cannot lead into greener pastures the sheep who have been cropping too long in one place if you have only been gleaning in that burned-over field yourself. When you take the pulpit to deliver the Word you were ordained to preach, let it be a real Word, and not something compounded in fever on Saturday night to be delivered in spasms on Sunday morning. From your arising on Monday morning, point your work and thoughts and emotions toward the performance of that singular duty on the next Sunday. Determine once and for all that you will set no instant puddings before your people, but that you shall provide them every time with a sane gospel immersed in life and fired by imagination.

Do that with some constancy and you will be surprised at the effect on your congregation. You will marvel at the way apathy gives way to eagerness and excitement. Businessmen and house-wives and schoolboys whom you believed to be completely and hermetically sealed off against the gospel will begin to put hard questions to you, friendship feelers from suspicious hearts, reeds in the wind to see how shifty you really are; and even before you know it, you will be caught up in a rhythm of reciprocity with them—a two-way tango—in which their prodding makes you preach better and your preaching makes them prod you more.

You will be astonished, moreover, at the change in yourself and in your ministry. Thitherto unrelated aspects of pastoral work and administrative labor and private rumination will suddenly one day begin to move into order. A structure to what you are doing will crystallize before your very eyes, so that you will see the multiple duties of your calling not as broken, tangled spokes, lying this way and that in hopeless disorder, but as parts of a solid and moving wheel, strongly supported and keenly ordered, and centering in upon that one true act, the preaching of the Word of God.

The priestly or liturgical aspect of the ministry, for example, will no longer seem a mere atavism, the embarrassing rain dance of the Arrow Collar society. On the contrary, it will appear in its true light as the collective action of a community celebrating the Word of grace at its center that has formed it and called it into being and provided the meaning for its total existence. Nor will the function of pastoral concern and counseling seem a thing apart, as though it ought to be performed under a secular shingle and not by the ministry; for preaching that is doing its proper work will ever and again become the basis of the counseling relationship, either because of what is said or because of the confidence that is there invoked in the counselor. Fosdick was right in saying that preaching is really an act of counseling *en masse,* because it is there that pastoral care ordinarily begins.

The same is true of Christian education; it too begins in the pulpit. As vital as the teaching ministry of the church is, it proceeds out of the kerygmatic utterance which brought the church into existence, and not the other way around. If it does not, then it tends to become either arrogant and imperial or irrelevant and futile. Even church administration, that facet of their professional involvement so many ministers loudly deplore, ought in real measure to reflect what is done in the pulpit, especially in the areas of moral principle, value judgment, personal relationships, and redemptive concern. A large church with a budget of several hundred thousands of dollars may well employ the services of a business manager, someone trained in finance and management, but woe unto any church that gives Caesar the governance over Christ even in so mundane a matter as the management of office personnel.

Finally, even the personal life of the minister and his family stands in an ineluctable and integral relationship to his preaching in the pulpit. The relationship may not be apparent at times, may not strike the casual observer as existing at all—and that is perhaps as it should be. But it is there. It is one of the physical laws of the world of our ministries, and we flout it at our own risk. We enrich and enliven both our preaching and our family joy by being aware of it and taking advantage of it the way a pilot takes advantage of a tailwind or a sailor of the tide and the currents.

Now this is not to say that the internal restructuring of the ministry happens easily or magically—that one random sermon with a happy conception and a fortunate kind of muscularity all the way to the end will make the various aspects of a man's ministry wheel to around it, the way the wilderness in Tennessee did around Wallace Stevens' jar. What is required is the *consistently* well-made sermon. There is a definite discipline involved, a weekly wrestling with a relevant text to produce a word that has gravity, that speaks, that means, that breathes of both contemporaneity and eternity. We cannot expect to come off cheaply in preaching about a Lord who suffered death among criminals. Ours is a long and painstaking work, an enterprise removed from tedium mainly to the extent that in that tedium we are continually experiencing our *Te Deums*. There is little place in the Christian ministry for men who keep what Dorothy Sayers once called "the Feast of St. Lazybones." It is an arduous, anguishing task to preach the gospel Sunday after Sunday, year after year, in ways that will not weary people, that will not betray them into thinking it flat and stale and repetitious. The only way to do it is to work at one's preaching with a deathless care.

In years of stricter ecclesiastical discipline, there was a practice in some churches of "fencing" the communion table—of warning away from it any who were considered unrepentant and unworthy of receiving the elements. One might almost wish there were a parallel act of fencing the pulpit today, of warding away from it any preacher who has not spent his ten or fifteen or twenty hours upon the sermon to be preached. For it is only in the matrix of great concern for preaching, in the loving development of the sermon through all its steps—from the careful exegesis of the text to the imaginative reflection which elicits from it a soundly organic outline; from the outline to the fulfillment of its promise in lively prose and apt illustration in the written sermon; and from the written sermon to the preachable sermon, that is in the heart and blood as well as in the mind—that we are ever able to achieve the desideratum which Professor John Knox has so appropriately called "the integrity of preaching."

It is impossible to overstress the importance of converting the sermon material into lively prose. Much of the so-called irrelevance of the contemporary pulpit is to be attributed more to banality and dullness of expression than anything else. Not that we always get into the pulpit with something to say. Unfortunately, we are too often guilty of the offense over which a Scottish woman is supposed to have twitted her minister, that he "hadna mickle to say and he dinna say it well." But a preacher may strike his course from the gospel every Sunday and, if he has not striven with the angel of language, fail.

Perhaps it is not so much the case as it was formerly, but it is still unfortunately true that most clergymen are regarded as the *orateurs d'occasion* of their communities and are called on to do everything from "commencerating" high schools to filling in for truant garden-club speakers. One minister of my acquaintance, who is also a theological professor, spoke a total of 252 times last year. At least that is what he told me; I find it nearly incredible. God may have given us unusual powers, but he has certainly not given us the power to flout the tables of multiplication and division. In proportion as a man multiplies his speeches and divides his energies, he diminishes his composure, his presence, his forcefulness as a preacher. Apparently the loquacious clergyman had never read the German poet Rainer Maria Rilke, who said, "One ought to wait and gather sense and sweetness a whole life long, and a long life if possible, and then, quite at the end, one might perhaps be able to write ten lines that were good."

He had not recognized that there is an integral relationship between words and sense, between sound and meaning, and that
one cannot be true so frequently, but must inevitably become a
parody of himself, and then a parody of himself becoming a
parody, and a parody of himself becoming a parody of a parody.

Most of us never in a lifetime learn to use words with, at the
same time, the kind of accuracy and control and imagination
that allows them to become truly sacramental bearers of the
Word of God. Not enough of us are aware of the sheer idolatry
involved in the common language of the pulpit. We never
realize that grace and incarnation are much more than our religious way of talking about them, that God is much more, that
the fellowship of believers is much more, that meaning and truth
and eternal life are always out beyond what we are saying at
the moment. It is surely a condemnation of our preaching, in an
age which has developed highly sophisticated philosophies of
semantics and linguistics, that we are doing less to make God
intelligible to people than almost any age before us. It is no
wonder there is a widespread apostasy from belief: we have
not provided belief its tools!

I have just read William Burroughs' non-novel *The Soft
Machine*. Skimmed is perhaps a better word; it is a repugnant
book, brimming with corruption and putrefaction, smelling of
feces and semen, impacted with perversion and death. But how
the prose flows! It sings and dances, lingers and leaps, pauses
and pirouettes, like a ballet or a Tivoli pantomime. What if
preachers, with their subject matter, I found myself thinking,
were to master their craft like this? Would the gospel not find
new tongues in this age, and new hearers? Would it not soar and
dip and hover in the public imagination once more? And wouldn't
the preacher himself thrill to the great chasms opening in what
he had thought was the bottom of faith, belief, mystery?

It is only as one struggles to articulate the Word, to find words
and ways of expressing it afresh at each presentation, that he
becomes fully aware of the mystery of it. In the exchange between
his words and the vivid Word that God has given, indeed con-

tinues to give, the preacher finds himself moving into realms he has never before visited; each sermon becomes a new experience in the nature of grace and the fact of revelation. T. S. Eliot said once of the English metaphysical poets that "a thought to them was an experience. It modified their sensibilities." The same ought to be true with the preacher. None of his sermons should leave him as he was. They ought to form themselves as he forms them and assume shapes he only partly intended, so that, in the end, they speak to him before they speak to anyone else. This is the greatness of true preaching. We do not make it ourselves; we discover it. It is like Pygmalion in reverse: as we work upon the inert material, we come suddenly, at some hidden point, to see that it is not really inert at all, but that we are, and that the compellingness of preaching is not in its becoming like us but in our becoming like it. Thus preaching becomes, issues in, is, revelation.

It is completely true, of course, as Barth has so insistently reminded us, that the only word which does our people any good is God's Word and not our word. But one has only to fancy speaking God's Word without using any words of his own (does this account for the persistence of King James English in pulpit speech?) to see how utterly between the horns he is. And it is the history of the pulpit that it has failed whenever it has chosen one horn over the other. Fundamentalism, for example, has usually tried to present "God's Word" with a minimum of concern for the best human words, and so has ended in enslavement to shibboleths; and liberalism, on the other hand, has at times been so concerned with human words and so unconcerned about their validation by a higher and more than human Word that it has finally lost sight of the transcendent in our midst.

But strive to make of the best human words a *larva,* a veil, a wardrobe for that world-ordering, destiny-altering, life-lifting Word that is over against, behind, and somehow in every good word spoken in its behalf, and you will discover the true and inimitable romance of preaching. You will become more and more aware, year by year, of the tremendous mystery in which you stand. The longer you preach, the greater the mystery will become for you. It will be like the waters in Ezekiel's vision: mystery to the ankles, slapping at the shins; then mystery to the knees, lapping at the thighs; then to the waist, crowding the chest; and finally there will be mystery like deep waters, enough to swim in; and you will find yourself like Alexander Whyte, when you are too old to mount a pulpit any longer, unable to forbear the pleasure of sitting at your desk every morning and working upon some new sermon, even though you know you will never preach it.

We are formed as we work at giving form to the Word of God. We become more and more like it as we study it and chisel at it and work it into our sermons; until at last, in rhythm with the Word that became flesh, our flesh in a very real sense becomes Word.

2

Preaching and Worship

One of the things today's advocates of dialogue-sermons appear to have forgotten in their haste to dump the more traditional form of the sermon is that good preaching, preaching that has been approached as poetry or revelation and then preached in at least a moderately acceptable fashion, approaches the level of incantation. It has a dramatic, ritualistic quality attainable only by a combination of skill and imagination, technique and inspiration. The more prosaic nature of the discussion or forum type of presentation is totally unsuitable to replace it. A poetry reading, a dance, a theatrical scenario, would be much more appropriate as a substitute; but they lack the sermon's Christian orientation, its directness, its "homing instinct."

But apparently it is not only the devotees of dialogue sermons who have forgotten the incantatory quality of good preaching; many preachers who labor week by week at the traditional kind of preaching ministry seem to have forgotten it too. In rural areas and in the churches of right-wing Protestantism this is not so true as it tends to be in urban centers and more liberal churches; there the ministers often depend heavily on a kind of instinctive rhythmic quality to their preaching and an affected tonality in their voices to create a state of semi-ecstasy in their congregations, usually in the absence of anything very sound or constructive to say. The two greatest recreations of the Negro sermon in literature, those of William Faulkner's *The Sound and the Fury* and Ralph Ellison's *Invisible Man,* reflect the innate power of the human voice, used in certain rhythmic and inflective patterns, to establish an almost trance-like rapport between the speaker and his audience. But the preaching one generally hears in more sophisticated churches today is quite tepid by comparison. It is almost as if the intelligent preachers were afraid of the techniques of persuasion, and were modeling their prose styles somewhere between Federalese (the language of official Washington) and Pedagogese (the unofficial but omniprevalent language of modern educators), so that they cannot really be accused of saying anything at all. They have become professional glibsters—which indicates perhaps as much as anything else the eclipse of belief in their lives.

The best preachers I have ever heard have been men with something significant to say which they said piquantly and poetically, with attention both to the manner of phrasing ideas and to the manner of speaking in which their sermons were delivered. They combined in their preaching the qualities of rhythm and rhetoric to be found in rural parsons who have little to say and of thought and intelligence to be found in professional theologians who can sometimes manage to seem as opaque and ponderous as peanut butter.

One of the most significant things about such preaching, apart from and yet somehow related to the content of the preaching, is its suitability to worship. Aesthetically, rhythmically, musically, dramatically, it is attuned to liturgy, so that it becomes a part of it, focalizes it, even enhances it. Far from seeming out of place in the solemnity of the service, in the lustiness of praise, the humility of confession, the joy of remembrance, it belongs, and *transubstantiates* these parts of the order into contemporary and meaningful experience.

Let me confess immediately that I am in profound accord with Evelyn Underhill when she speaks of that "despotism of the pulpit" which has in so many instances characterized Protestant worship—a despotism which has resulted in the average layman's regarding the prayers and praise and even the reading of the Scriptures as mere "preliminaries" in the service, and Communion as an occasional rite to be suffixed to the principal trunk of the worship at the discretion of the minister or by an accident of the calendar. (Occasionally even some minister is heard to announce the observance of the Lord's Supper *after* the worship hour!) The indomitable growth of the sermon in the service during the eighteenth and nineteenth centuries, like that of the legendary camel which kept drinking water and expanding until she had filled her owner's tent and had finally crowded everybody else off the oasis, has had a generally regrettable effect upon worship in Protestant churches, and one that will not soon be remedied or erased.

If I speak here of the centrality of the sermon in worship, I do so in the highest sense possible and with full regard for the total pattern, the *Gestalt,* of worship. I mean that the sermon, properly conceived and effectually preached, is the point of focus which gives true depth and shading and meaning to the rest of the picture, so that nothing in the service—not the subtlest phrasing of a prayer or the slightest tremor of praise—is lost or undervalued. The sermon is to the Christian order of service what the matter of perspective is to drawing and painting. It is the place where the hearer, like the viewer in art, discovers his most intimate personal relationship to the whole, where he discovers his stance, where he finds himself most engaged, most in tension, with what is happening. From there, both backward and forward —back to the Call to Worship or the opening hymn and forward to the Benediction—everything unfolds and assumes its proper meaning.

The basic assumption of such an analogy is that the sermon is the place in the service where the Word that is beyond all words, even beyond the sermon, stares through most nakedly at us, where, as Dante describes a particularly luminous passage in his *Purgatorio,* "the veil now is indeed so thin, that of a surety to pass within is easy." As the influence of a sound liturgy safeguards preaching from becoming mere exhibitionism or illuminism (witness the negative situation in many aliturgical churches), it is the influence of sound preaching that imparts to the liturgy a sense of the existential and contemporaneous.

This is not to say that the other items of the service may not be existential. But the very fact that we speak of the *Word* of God indicates that something passes from one person to another —that revelation and redemption are highly personal; and the Word of God rarely becomes more personal than when it is being mediated in, through, or by the means of the human voice in the act of preaching. What is it that Joan of Arc says in Shaw's play when someone tells her that the voices she hears are not God, but her imagination? "Of course. That is how the messages of God come to us." And is there any place in the entire order of Christian worship where the imagination is more primed and piqued (or ought to be) for the voices of God than in the sermon? The worshiper may be keenly aware of the whole service, taking it on tiptoes, so to speak, so that no iota of it is really lost upon him; but let the minister step into the pulpit to preach and he feels a sudden tightening in the breast, a sudden sense of excitement, as if the most wonderful thing were about to happen. It is here that the great drama becomes intensely personal, intensely his, gripping him, transfixing him, holding him awestruck by the unveiling of truth in his very presence. If he is a sensitive person, and the sermon is very good, he will not get over it for days, but will carry with him the feeling of what has happened, of what has come to pass in his life in a moment of worship.

Literary critics, especially those accustomed to dealing in what is known as *explication de texte,* sometimes speak of the *point* of a passage or a story or a poem, by which they mean not the message the author wishes to impart but that certain half-spatial interpretative center of the piece, from which the real union of form and matter in the writing emerges and begins to unravel.

The sermon is such a point in the service of worship. It is the place where form and matter really become one in the consciousness of the congregation, where the faith that is celebrated by ritual and by rendering of praise suddenly comes home and is real in the depths, lending reality and unity to the rest of the service.

What happens when preaching ceases to be this point, this center-making interweaver of magic and meaning, can be seen in the history of the Roman liturgy and its long deliverance into automatism. Everything in the service calcifies, becomes fixed, habitual, boring. Even priests themselves have frequently confessed to a kind of boredom in the execution of their rituals. They may begin their careers as young clergymen with tremulous sensitivity to what is supposed to occur as they elevate the Host in the Mass—John Osborne has caught this delicate moment in his play about Luther, when the young Augustinian monk is about to serve his first Communion—but ordinarily the whole business soon deteriorates into a perfunctory thing, an obligation they cannot wait to be done with.

We must be careful not to minimize, on the other hand, the danger in concentrating too exclusively on the sermon and having less than a proper regard for the great liturgical acts which through the centuries have reminded worshipers of their place in the *communio sanctorum,* in the body of saints through all the ages. Not for a minute should we argue for the kind of *logos*olatry which has in numerous Protestant communions replaced the liturgiology they so despised in the Roman church. It is too dry, too brittle, too lacking in the concept of Incarnation. It betrays us in the end to a kind of docetism of the Word, where any idea of its becoming flesh or really penetrating the quiddity, the essence, of this world is almost totally shunned.

Professor Hugh T. Kerr has analyzed our dilemma, our double-pronged or double-sided problem, in a little monograph entitled *Mystery and Meaning in the Christian Faith.* First he notes the connection in the thinking of St. Paul between the use of the word "mystery" and the task of proclaiming the gospel;

the two are really inseparable. Then he examines both the Roman and the Protestant churches for the manner in which they have continued to recognize the indivisibility of mystery and proclamation. What he sees is this: The Roman church has on one hand made mystery more mysterious, indeed almost miraculous, by minimizing the element of proclamation (this monograph was written before the present movement of renewal in the Roman communion); and the Protestant fellowship, on the other hand, has in its general obsession with the business of preaching quite lost the sense of mystery. The two have thus formed separate ends of a spectrum. What is more needed, concludes Professor Kerr, is a return to the middle, a reinvestment of Romanism with the significance of a plain-spoken gospel, and of Protestantism with a due sense of the *mysterium tremendum,* the inscrutable otherness of the Holy that is finally impervious to human logic or understanding.

It is heartening to see at the present time in both communions a belated repentance for the loss of one or the other of the two elements and a movement, even if the movement sometimes resembles a confused scramble or a game of musical chairs *à l'église,* toward the recovery of what has been neglected. There is considerable excitement among some avant-garde Protestants over the rediscovery of liturgical principles, issuing in a spate of books and magazine articles on the subject, and, in many churches, a kind of higgledy-piggledy reinstitution of medieval practices (at this point we are far more willing to go backwards than we are to go forwards). There is similar jubilance among certain Catholic groups for a renaissance of sound biblical preaching, which has on its side of the fence already resulted in the publication of a periodical called *Preaching* and in numerous conferences on the homiletical malaise and what can be done about it. The combination of prophecy and temple worship, which was in a sense effected already in Jewish synagogue worship but became the staple of Christian worship in the early centuries, bids fair to return again in both Roman and non-Roman settings.

If a guideline is wanted to steer us through the tricky channels of this reordering process, it may be that there is still no sounder principle than that voiced by Luther, who, after all, stood at the division of the ways still in Catholic territory, and is even today beginning to be accepted by many Catholics as a *Catholic* reformer who was so hard-headed that he "sacrificed unity for truth" (the words are those of Fr. Daniel Morrissey, a Dominican priest who preached the Reformation Day sermon in the American Church of Paris on October 29, 1967, celebrating the 450th anniversary of Luther's posting of the Ninety-Five Theses). "This is the sum of the matter," wrote Luther, "that everything shall be done so that the Word prevails."

Luther was by no means such a radical spirit as we sometimes conceive him to be. The words "I cannot do otherwise," though probably of spurious origin, are really an accurate mark of his predicament; he did not wish to break with Rome, but his conscience was closer to him than Rome was. Jonathan Swift caught him precisely in that delightful little story *A Tale of a Tub,* where Martin, repentant in spirit over having embellished with a free hand the coat his father bequeathed him with instructions to keep it plain, gently removes some of the gaudier appurtenances, while his brother Jack (Calvin) enthusiastically removes everything from his garment, rending it quite hopelessly in the process, and his brother Peter (the Pope) busies himself with gathering up anything and everything the other brothers discard and sewing it onto his already overly ornate vestment. What Luther wanted was not to destroy the liturgy of the Catholic church but to reinvest it with meaning by restoring the predominance of the Word. Not for a minute did he intend that the Word should usurp the place of the liturgy, but that it should inform it and infuse it with significance and meaning for every worshiper.

Of course the Word did not mean to Luther only the act of preaching or the act of reading the Scriptures in the vernacular. It meant the Spirit of God, the living Word, the inspiring Word, whose presence alone brings meaning either to Scripture or to preaching. Yet that living Word, for Luther, worked nowhere more actively than in the word preached from the pulpit by a man standing firmly on a sound biblical text. It was here, in the sermon, that God really danced a joy-dance of redemption and reconciliation.

What Luther really insisted on, in other words, was the centrality of the sermon in worship, not with the implication that the other items in the service are thereby diminished in importance, but, on the contrary, that they are heightened and exalted to their true status only as the sermon brings the Word from beyond to bear upon them and illumine them, actualizing them and contemporizing them to the specific congregation gathered to participate in them.

Although I am not myself an advocate of the central pulpit in church architecture, I am inclined to believe that R. W. Dale had more than a nineteenth-century idiosyncrasy on his side of the argument when he protested to Principal Fairbairn of Mansfield College in Oxford that it was unfitting to place the pulpit at the side of the college's new chapel. "I wonder," he wrote, "what would be said of architect and building committee, if after they had erected a concert hall, a fiddler could be heard only when he stood in a corner." Dale wanted to put into practice architecturally what Luther had called for in spirit.

By this time the stricter liturgiologist reading this probably has a grimace on his face that would frighten some of the gargoyles on Notre Dame Cathedral. I can almost read his mind: "The Communion, as the traditional dramatic fulfillment of the worship experience, is by rights the central act and the objective point of reference for everything else in the liturgy; it cannot be crowded out by preaching, no matter how good or how pertinent." If that is so, let me relieve him by saying that I agree, there is a sense in which he is correct. Like Othello's murdering of Desdemona in Shakespeare's play, the Rite of the Table is the climax of all that has gone before, or rightly should be. In the Communion, all the senses are assaulted by the Word: auditory, visual, tactile, even the olfactory, if it is keen. On a very good day its effects can in fact be similar to those described by users of LSD who have been on a trip and have "seen" music and "smelled" color and "touched" beauty and achieved other syn-esthetic feats (did Augustine have something like this in mind when he described the sacraments as "visible words"?). It is, without doubt, the high moment in the service, the one we have all waited for.

But without a sermon to interpret it, without a proclaimed word to produce the initial encounter, without the coming of Christ again in the spoken word, none of the more significant aspects of the Communion will be present. There will be no eucharist, or paean of thanksgiving; no real anamnesis, or re-constituting of the Lord's presence; no genuine communion, either with God or among the people; and the principal sense of mystery will be that debased one of the later Middle Ages against which the Reformers protested so vigorously that it was a magical act and a "dumb show." The early Nonconformists in England were right in insisting (and it was in their heritage that Dale stood) on the priority of two pieces of furniture in their meeting houses, a pulpit and a table, the one for the Word and the other for the sacrament. But the pulpit was raised above the table to bespeak the absolute primacy of the Word in wor-ship. Tall and neck-craning, it commanded the central view, and reminded the worshipers without fail that nothing, not even a sacrament, is sacramental and grace-bearing without "the true and lively Word."

Lest it be complained that this emphasis is greatly unfair to the sacramental aspect of worship, I must hasten to add that the converse is also true, that the Word without the sacrament is incomplete, that it is truncated and aborted, that it has not reached its proper fulfillment. Calvin called the sacraments *sigilla verbi divini*—seals of the divine Word—and they are that indeed. They carry into the senses what has been proposed to the mind and heart. And if we are at all Hebraic in our psychology, and see a true relation between soul and body, then we cannot but consider the sacraments as preaching carried a step beyond itself, so that it addresses the whole of our being and not just a part.

It would be a good test for any sermon to ask if it might be followed immediately by the Lord's Supper without jarring the aesthetic and emotional sensibilities of the finest and most discerning souls in the congregation. If so, then the sermon may be judged to be doing its proper work of bringing Christ again to the people. If not, a further examination is called for. Perhaps the sermon is too coldly intellectual to lead directly into the sacrament. Perhaps it is too lacking in *kerygma,* in rehearsal of what is always at the heart of the Christian gospel, so that it seems out of place with the sacrament which embodies as its symbolic nucleus the saving acts of God. Perhaps it is arrogant and humanistic, so as to be disconsonant with the gospel of grace, of which the sacrament is the enduring safeguard. Or perhaps the sermon is even aridly programmatic, as is so often the case in my own denomination, and thus forbids the congregation's entrance upon such holy ground. This test will tell, and will keep a minister on course in his preaching. Even when there is to be no Communion, the sermon may well be an ante-Communion one, suitable as preparation for that dramatic act, so that God may most fully mediate to men his own spiritual communion and presence.

Word *and* sacrament—that was the keynote of the Reformation, and it should be even better understood from our own perspective in the twentieth century, for now we have seen where an overemphasis on either aspect will lead. We have followed it into the barren preachathons of Protestantism and into the objectionable objectivity of the Roman Mass. And we should be ready, more than the churchmen of any other era since the first, for a creative reciprocity between the Word in preaching and the Word in sacrament.

Theoretically of course it is the responsibility of the whole people of God, the *laos tou theou,* to keep alive the dramatic relationship between Word and sacrament; but practically it becomes the business of the minister. He, perforce, lives with it in the most intimate way. As Dom Gregory Dix observes frankly in *The Shape of the Liturgy,* the laity are often grossly indifferent to liturgy except as it pleases or displeases them. It is the minister who must be its servant, who must be constantly sensitizing the souls of his people to it, who must preserve it from becoming a mere holy dance or superstitious ritual, by keeping it in tension with the Word of God. Our people may be largely apathetic about liturgical matters, but we who preach cannot afford to be. And, unless I am greatly mistaken, it is the degree to which we appreciate the true nature of evangelical preaching that finally determines how careful we shall be in the leadership of worship.

If we faithfully discharge our priestly duties as the entrepreneurs of worship, as the stage managers and producers and directors of the service of worship, we will strive to keep the service and the sermon always in proper tension, so that the sermon itself is an integral part of worship and continually flashes its light both backward and forward, drawing the apparently disparate and discrete parts of the liturgy into order and unity.

A good sermon is like the host at a great party, whose conversation with the guests puts them at ease with one another and provides the integrating center around which they discover relationship and without which they would be only so many individuals grouped in the same room. The host—the sermon—is the catalyst. Here is a businessman who even in church cannot put business out of his head: he is in no mood for a confession of sin. Here is a distraught housewife trying to restrain a wiggly four-year-old from marking in the hymnal: she would be the first to admit that she is not getting much from the Scripture lessons. Here is an old man with a heart condition now rather intent on feeling his pulse: he will not enter very enthusiastically into the spirit of the *Sursum Corda.* Here is a pretty slip of a girl who has caught the eye of a pleasant looking lad: it's a safe bet that the benediction will not mean very much to her except as a prelude to courtship maneuvers. But the sermon catches all their moods and winds them about and provides the relationship and internal meaning to all the varied items of worship, reflecting upon each the glory which truly belongs to it but was not seen; and the businessman, the housewife, the old fellow with a heart condition, and the girl with stars in her eyes all go out strangely warmed by having been "in the house of the Lord."

It is in the preaching, more than in any other part of worship, that the service fails or succeeds. As Ronald Knox said in that remarkable chatty and graceful little book *The Mass in Slow Motion,* the leader of worship is like a magnifying glass catching and focusing the radiant presence of God upon the tinder of the congregation's devotion, so that warmth and fire are produced in the very heart of the service. And it is in the sermon that he has the hugest opportunity of kindling the sparks into a bonfire, of bringing to steady heat what has been felt only as isolated pressure or inclination of temperature. This is not to say that the minister should not be vitally concerned with the total program of worship, with prayer and praise and psalm, with canticle and contribution and Communion; indeed he should be ever restless to improve the order of service both as to its larger movements and to its preciser ingredients. It is to say, however, that there is no place more logical or more profitable for the minister to begin his improvements upon congregational worship than in the fifteen or twenty minute slot occupied each Sunday morning by his own sermon, for, given the character of the relationship between preaching and worship, there is no other place so vital.

I was in a certain Northern city once for several weeks, and generally on Sunday went for worship to the magnificent chapel of the city's most outstanding university. I still shiver with excitement to recall the tremendous music produced by the choir and organ each time I was there. Often I was literally entranced by it, so enthralled that the minister's voice at prayer time or at sermon time would suddenly disturb me from deep revery. As it was during an interim period when the chapel had no senior minister, the associate minister composed the variables of the service and led in the worship; and he did a superlative job, choosing hymns and reading the lessons and offering prayers that were surprisingly on a par with the majestic music. But as there was no regular minister, the business of preaching fell to this person and that, to academic conventioners and name-brand clergymen and local theologians; and it was the greatest fiasco imaginable. "Have sermon, will travel." Again and again the great service moved forward, building always in anticipation and intensity to the time of the sermon, only then to fall flat on its face and grovel epileptically for thirty minutes or more while some poor dull fellow labored with increasing despair to pull off a deal that had probably worked very well back in his home town, or even reasonably well in the small college setting where he had preached the Sunday preceding. Only rarely did a preacher come along—Tillich was one of them, with a sermon on hope—who was a match for the service, who could go beyond it and make the fires burn brightly, who could make one think he was at Pentecost again. And on all the other occasions that remarkable service (for when do they ordinarily hang together so well on their own?) was practically ruined, at least certainly vitiated, by preaching that did not begin to test the limits of its own possibility, that did not become "true and lively" by any measure of the words. It fell in a shambles and left the congregation dour and disappointed because the promise of a word, of a happening in the pulpit, had not been fulfilled. There is the problem we have been talking about turned the other way around, where the service almost made it on its own but fell through because the preaching was poor.

Either way, it ought to be apparent that preaching and worship make one claim upon the minister, not two, and that the clearest, surest way for him to begin the revitalization and improvement of worship among his people is through the revitalization and improvement of his own sermons, which stand both theologically and practically at the center of true worship. Ask any group of laymen. They will be blunt about it. They admit that the liturgy might stand some revisions, though they tend to be hesitant about change in areas of custom and tradition.

But they are all sure of one thing, and that is that they could do with much better preaching than they are hearing, and wish any reform in worship might begin right there.

"I wish he would stop moving the candlesticks and start concentrating on his sermons," said one man of his pastor. "If he spent half the time on his pulpit notes that he spends fiddling with the order of service, he would be another Billy Graham. [The man was a Southern fundamentalist.] We never get anything done in deacons' meeting for his wanting to propose some new change and everybody else's being opposed to it. Consequently he thinks we're all against him and he gets his feelings hurt too easily. How do you tell a preacher that the trouble is not in the service, it's in him?" And then the man went on to expatiate for fifteen minutes or so on the homiletical *faux pas* the minister had committed during his sermon the preceding Sunday morning.

I know another minister, on the other hand, whose preaching has been so good that he has done whatever he wished with the service. And once one of the elders in his church came to him and said, "Preacher, our choir tries hard, but it's not the Fred Waring Singers. Some of us think it may be a little hard for you to preach right after them. We were thinking that maybe if we moved the anthem back before the offering it would make things easier for you."

Professor John A. Broadus knew what he was talking about several years ago when he said that the Reformation, before it was anything else, was a reformation of preaching; and, on the practical level, it will be the same with any kind of reformation in our churches today that is significant and enduring.

It is humiliating that this should be so, especially in regard to worship, because (as Jean-Jacques von Allmen has observed in his tight-lipped little volume on *Preaching and Congregation*) of all the elements on the agenda of public worship, none is so completely subject to the idiosyncrasies and personal abuse of the officiating minister. We all have listened to preachers who made us wish with all our power that it might befall them as it befell a certain Zacharias, of whom Luke records that an angel confronted him, saying, "Thou shalt be dumb and not able to speak." But this no more gainsays the work of a true sermon than the incoherent mumblings of a parrot-priest invalidate the real worth of the ancient liturgy.

Subjectivism in the pulpit is no grave danger when the church understands the limitations of any one man's instrumentation of the gospel and when the minister rightly apprehends his responsibility as the spokesman of the church, when he realizes that he is only the spearpoint reaching into the present moment to impale it with the weight and thrust of the whole spear and shaft of the entire communion of the saints in all the ages behind him. In *The Public Worship of God* Henry Sloan Coffin quotes this memorable paragraph on preaching, taken from a description by G. A. Johnston Ross of his visit to the little abbey on the island of Iona, off the coast of Scotland, where Columba founded a college of preachers in the sixth century. The abbey had been restored on the very altar foundation where Columba worshiped and died, and Ross was to preach there.

> As I took my place at the little temporary pulpit beside the ancient altar base [said Ross], and looked first at my congregation (composed in part of scientific men from England, in part of the aged fishermen whom I had known as stalwart lads) and then through the glassless windows at the burial place of sixty-six of our Scottish and Norwegian kings and earls, whose bodies a thousand years ago had been brought there because of the sanctity of the holy isle, there swept over me (need you wonder?) an awe of the Eternal who had labored so long within the aspirations of men . . . . What I preached that day is long ago forgotten, as is most meet; but I shall never forget what I *was* that day—consciously the child of the centuries and of the variegated grace of God which they carried. All petty provincialism was impossible: the broken altar base, the stern lift of the walls, the presence of the august dead, forbade. And this elevation of soul and broadening of view do come to the men who appreciate the presence of God in the community of faith.

No man, feeling like that, can ever be despotic or eccentric in the pulpit, for he realizes with a flooding sense of poignancy and humility that he is no mere peripatetic voice, taking his stand where he pleases, but a minister of God and an ordinand of the universal church.

There is no substitute for preaching in worship. It provides the proclamatory thrust without which the church is never formed and worship is never made possible. It complements the creedal, poetic nature of the liturgy and keeps before men the absolute contemporaneity of the gospel, as of a Word made always present and personal to them under the pressure of their current life-situations. It sharpens our perception for the mystery of Communion, which properly climaxes all Christian worship, and it thereby makes possible a true and meaningful sacramentalism. It forbids mere ritualism and automatism in the service by continually inserting into worship the presence of a new and unique word, one which is never quite the same again when preached in another setting or published in a compendium of sermons. Above all, it provides better than anything else the necessary encounter between the lackadaisical worshiper and the intensity of Christ's lordship. It, of all the elements in the liturgy, is primary, for it and it alone is able to guarantee the success of Christian worship and the Christian sacraments.

Preaching is the Little Scandal corresponding to the Greater Scandal of our Lord's having come himself as a Word in the flesh: though it be open to the most dismal failure (how far, through twenty million star-studded miles of space, have some sermons fallen flat and plopped soufflé-like on a chancel step!), it is open also to the most incredible success. Nowhere else, either in worship or the wide, wide world, does God confront us so directly, probe us so relentlessly, or mediate himself to us so intoxicatingly, as he does in the preaching of his Word.

Therefore the minister pauses when he gets into the pulpit, pauses and reflects on the terrible gravity of the thing he is about to do—speak in the name of God. He has an impulse to run and hide, to cover his head before the hills fall upon him, for he

knows his speech is too little, too banal, too dreadfully impover-
ished ever to represent the majesty or the truth of God's own
speech. If only he could confess his fear to the congregation,
could say to them, "There will be no sermon this morning, or
ever again as far as this preacher is concerned, for the law that
is written not on tables of stone but on the heart is a flabby
thing, an elusive thing, and I am never sure when I have got
hold of it." But he can't. He knows he can't. They are out there
waiting. Those upturned faces with the waiting eyes belong to
men and women who have hung their hope on the preacher,
who are always haunted by the anticipation of a word, who are
desperate to have a report from what Barth calls "the other side
of life." He cannot betray them; better betray God than them.
And in the betrayal that takes place Sunday by Sunday, he becomes ever more scared, ever more afraid that he is misleading
them, that he is replacing the gospel with words of his own that
have no power to save and no truth to ennoble. Only occasionally, in the increasingly rare moments of dramatic renewal in
his own faith and life, is he vouchsafed the sudden inexplicable
confidence that somehow, mysteriously, his broken, stammered
words have been touched and transmuted into the Word of God
for those people—have been life and breath, body and blood, to
them. Then, sighing deeply, he gives thanks, looks at the world
with newly wondering eyes, and hitches up his belt to begin again.

He is the actor in center stage; many men speak well of him,
and that is a liability. But he knows that he is not alone in his
performance, that there is a sense in which he depends heavily
upon the rest of the cast when he plays his part, and will be good
or bad according to how well or ill they perform theirs. The
audience is important, for some are like cold spaghetti, stiff and
rubbery, and cannot be played to, while others are warm and
receptive, keyed to respond to the deftest remark, the slightest
innuendo. And even during a good performance, when the
breaks fall right and the supporting cast is on cue and the
audience is enthusiastic and alert, eliciting the best that is in a
man, the actor and the audience both know, in a kind of un-

spoken pact between them, that there is something else, that these are not all the ingredients, that behind the phantasmagoria of lights and effects there is a play and there is a playwright, and that it is *his* success that is celebrated in the theater, *his* word that is heard, *his* play that is played.

Especially if you go to the theater knowing the playwright, versed in his ideas by previous plays, by interviews and articles, is it true that you find yourself adoring him, revering him, worshiping him, as the play proceeds, and not the actors and actresses who speak his lines or move his movements. It is his hour, not theirs; and your pleasure at their fluency and facility is only a secondary pleasure, an ancillary benefit, for the play is the thing and the playwright is the one who made the thing, who dreamed it and birthed it and gave it the life that it has.

How important it is that the actor remember this constantly—the actor in God's drama, I mean—and that he subordinate his talent and his energy and his personality to the whole play, to the message and the impact of the one behind the play. He has the best lines, by and large, in the entire play; if they were removed there wouldn't be a play. But they are not his to run away with, not his as his own personal property, not his as though he had made them by himself. They belong to the playwright, first of all, and to the play and to the rest of the cast and last but not least to the audience, to those for whom the play was conceived, for whom the playwright sweat drops of blood, for whom he died a little bit in bringing the play into existence.

Knowing this, the actor, the preacher, the man in middle stage, will not blunt his potential by dreaming of himself as a prima donna; and on the other hand, he will stand and speak his lines with courage, for they are not really his at all, but his who made the play.

And the play, as anyone knows, is the thing.

3

PREACHING AND PASTORAL CARE

When the history of the twentieth century pulpit in America is written it is doubtful that any figure in it will loom larger than that of Harry Emerson Fosdick, the famous minister of Riverside Church in New York City. No man's sermons have been given wider attention by radio and newspaper reporters, by professors and theologians, by doctors and lawyers and businessmen, or by students of preaching and other ministers. For years, what Fosdick said from the pulpit in Riverside on Sunday morning became the subject of news releases, classroom discussions, and other men's sermons the following week.

Yet Fosdick regarded himself more as a counselor than as a preacher, defining his sermons as "personal counseling on a group scale." He spoke in his autobiography, *The Living of These Days,* of having a monumental distrust for any minister who thinks of the sermon as the crux of his ministry. The temptations of the popular preacher are too great, he felt—to preach "successful" sermons, to exult in the adulation of crowds, to substitute rhetoric and eloquence (and even subtle exhibitionism) for real inspiration, and to be seduced into thinking of himself far more highly than he ought. The only thing that can save a gifted preacher from these ever-present and difficult-to-recognize temptations is a genuine care for persons, so that when the preacher is in a crowd, the one thing that matters to him beyond all others is to get in touch, vitally in touch, with some individual.

Fosdick's own prayer as he got up to preach was always, "Somewhere in this congregation is one person who desperately needs what I am going to say; O God, help me to get at him!"

This subordination of the pulpit to the ministry of personal counseling, coming from such a distinguished preacher, is not hard to swallow. Indeed, it comes as a welcome corrective to the sort of oratorical pulpitizing we inherited from earlier generations, whose supreme disregard for persons was evidenced by the length of the sermons as well as by either the bombastic or the essayistic subject matter of most of them. Fosdick himself spent a distressing apprenticeship to the older methods of preaching before he discovered the advantages and excitement of the kind of preaching for which we know him.

But Fosdick was a giant among preachers, a Paul Bunyan of the pulpit who felled great timber every time he took his ax in hand. What about all the ordinary men, the little preachers, the pygmy pulpiteers who have tried to imitate him? These, unfortunately, have not always been able to hold preaching and counseling in the same sort of tension that Fosdick held them in in his unusual ministry. They have not had the knee-knocking, hand-trembling, voice-quavering experience of facing that international and interdenominational crowd of worshipers at Riverside Church and trying to preach a sermon that could hold its own as a sermon regardless of whatever group counseling was in it. They have not had to stand and make their weekly presentations in front of learned professors and doctors and preachers from all over the globe, knowing that their homilies would be discussed and criticized and autopsied in the seminaries and universities as well as at the Sunday dinner table. And they have tended therefore to allow counseling to nudge out preaching in their

ministries and to think of the sermon as a necessary evil which
the masses in the church will be willing for them to abandon
once the masses have been educated to the importance of the
individual conference or the small-group therapy session.

I am exaggerating, of course; the relaxation of the creative
tension is not generally so pronounced as this. But it is becoming
a problem. In the United States, especially, exponents of counseling have more and more undermined the significance of the
pulpit ministry, implying that it is at best an inferior method of
working with individuals. In their preoccupation with the materials and methods of psychology they have frequently given the
impression that they are not really concerned with theology or
the Bible except as these in their faltering ways are able to sub-
stantiate the theories and insights of psychoanalysis. Fosdick himself has appeared to be vulnerable at this point, and has drawn
repeated attacks for having diluted the evangelical and kerygmatic aspects of the preaching ministry.

As one critic has contended, the average counselor tends to
view the content of the Christian faith as "a 'resource,' a kind of
medicine bag from which the skillful practitioner may select the
psychologically acceptable potions (such as 'forgiveness' and
'acceptance') which will best facilitate his real business of symp-
tomatic relief and therapy."[1] Pastoral care, says this critic, has
come increasingly to regard the faith more as a medicine to be
prescribed than as a message to be proclaimed. It is therapeu-
tically and not kerygmatically oriented.

The counselor's dilemma is understandable. Whether the
technique he employs in private conferences is directive or non-
directive, it must at least be characterized as very permissive. He
can in no way afford to seem judgmental. He cannot even fall
immediately on his knees and say, "Let's pray about it," for
that is to betray the fact that an inner arbitration of the case has
already taken place. The counselee must feel completely free to
divulge the darkest secrets of a corrupt or confused personality

[1] Frederic Wood, "Kerygma and Therapy: The Pastor's Dilemma," *Union
Seminary Quarterly Review,* XVIII, No. 2 (January, 1963), 123-124.

without fear of reprisal or recrimination. And until this kind of rapport or confidence is established, the counselor cannot do a truly effective work. Yet, merely by being associated with the formalized ministry, he is thought to be not only a judge but an accuser and a prosecutor as well. He is stigmatized by centuries of tradition in which the minister was regarded as the super-ego of the community, the black-robed voice of conscience who wiggled his finger and waggled his tongue at every form or suspicion of human vice. This is an unfortunate association which the minister cannot overcome by appearing in bermudas at the annual church picnic or playing shortstop in the local ball league or telling earthy stories at civic club dinners. The old cry of the children racing through the house, "Parson's coming! Parson's coming!" still precedes him wherever he goes. It is almost a part of the racial unconscious.

It is perhaps little wonder then that some ministers who are serious about their work in private counseling cringe a bit whenever they enter the pulpit, for the pulpit, set in front of the entire congregation at a height at least slightly above them, is the most formal identification the minister has with the continuance of the ministerial tradition from generation to generation. The very fact that he gets into the pulpit means that he has put a distance between himself and the few dozens of people with whom he has had intimate consultations—a distance he must try again to overcome the next time he is in conference with these persons.

So if a minister tries in the pulpit to sound as untheological and unchurchly—even *anti*theological and *anti*churchly—as possible, this may be the reason. He is trying to stay on the level of personal confidence with the people he must meet on a private basis during the week, and to do it he is willing even to sacrifice his appearance as a *keryx* or official agent of the gospel and become a bootlegger of the gospel. He does not intentionally put therapy ahead of kerygma, as the critic I have quoted suggests. He sees it as a matter of a different method, not of a different content. But he would not deny with any vehemence that his ministry is far more suggestive than assertive, and that the trumpet he is supposed to blow may frequently sound as uncertain as the orchestration of various humanistic and psychological approaches to the salvation of man.

It is against this general background that we have received the thought of a man like Eduard Thurneysen, a longtime friend and confident of theologian Karl Barth who has puzzled for years over how the insights expressed by Barth (many of them were Thurneysen's before they were Barth's, exchanged by the fireside on long winter evenings) become relevant and dynamic in the pastoral ministry.

The main transition to be made, says Thurneysen, is from Barth's emphasis on the *holiness* of God to the corresponding emphasis on the *forgiveness* of God. The two must be kept in indissoluble tension. They are the God-side and the human-side of the same thing. God is holy and we have offended his holiness; but the gospel we have received is the news that God has forgiven the offense and wishes to receive men again through Jesus Christ. Our primary task as ministers is to make this known to people. What we are called to is, above everything else, a ministry of reconciliation.

There is not really a bifurcation of purpose between preaching the gospel and counseling with the gospel. They are both concentric upon the fact of forgiveness, and overlie one another. But—and Thurneysen pounds this home again and again—it is preaching that is intensest at the very center of the ministry of reconciliation, with pastoral care as its extension into the individual lives of the congregation. Where this is not so, he says, pastoral care will make a futile attempt to replace the sermon and the sacraments—futile because they are its only *raison d'être*. Preaching and pastoral care have the same content; in the first instance the content takes a public form, and in the second a private. Or, as P. T. Forsyth said in *Positive Preaching and the Modern Mind,* "The pastor is only the preacher in retail."

Can the reader see the difference between this view of the preaching-counseling relationship and the view which Fosdick had? It is a subtle difference, but perhaps an important one.

Both views see a profound accord between the two aspects of ministry, and to a casual observer the two may appear to be very similar. But the significant distinction has to do with the starting point of the ministry itself. In Fosdick's view, the sermon begins with its own object: the people who need it. He was unabashed in his admission of this. But in Thurneysen's view the heavier emphasis—only slightly heavier—is on the divine initiation of the redemptive act, on God's recognition of man's need and his moving to meet that need. There is no apology for being theocentric in the matter. Indeed, it is recognized that there is no health apart from God, that our being away from him is the prime source of our problems anyway, and that we can do nothing better than hear proclaimed the message of his acceptance of us in spite of our problems. Humanity is not lost sight of; the gospel is seen to exist solely for its benefit. But there is never any doubt where the center is, and what is the measure of things: it is God!

A valid understanding of man and his deepest need is to be gained only from the Scriptures, says Thurneysen. "Man is created by the Word of God; thus, he can only be perceived in faith through the Word of God. Here the spiritual and the purely natural knowledge of human nature part ways. True pastoral care must be *biblical*. Let it beware of deviating from this! It proceeds from faith, but it also leads to faith. For man is created not only by the Word, but also for the sake of the Word. It follows that our care for man can consist in nothing else than in announcing the Word to him. To care for man means to provide him with this Word. Proclamation of the Word is therefore the beginning and the end of all true pastoral care." [2]

There is the principle we are after that will safeguard both preaching and pastoral care and keep them in harmonious relationship: proclamation, that hazardous, breathtaking, system-defying speaking of a Word into life, stands at the center of our calling to be ministers of God; it naturally has both a public

---

[2] Eduard Thurneysen, *A Theology of Pastoral Care* (Richmond: John Knox Press, 1962), p. 66.

and a private side, and the private side depends upon the public both for its beginning and its consummation.

To speak thus of the primacy of preaching is not to say that preaching is in any way independent of pastoral care. On the contrary, there is a vital relationship between the two, and the preacher who scorns the working out of the Word in the lives of his people will soon find himself speaking a haughty and irrelevant word from the pulpit.

Consider the contributions which a proper attitude toward pastoral discipline and pastoral care (they do not always seem the same to us as they did to Calvin) invariably makes to our preaching.

For one thing, it keeps people in our sight as the objects of God's love and redemptive activity, and therefore imbues our preaching with the larger human sympathies. Fosdick was quite right in deriding the preacher who "proceeds still upon the idea that folk come to church desperately anxious to discover what happened to the Jebusites." [3] The geometrical description of preaching is an ellipse, not a circle, with two foci, not one: God *and* persons. Our preaching is for people. It is *from* God (that is our high hope), but it is *for* people. And no preacher can succeed at his job who does not basically love people and want the gospel to mean something to them at their own private levels of understanding and receptivity. He may write out and deliver so-called "great" sermons; they may look good in a book that sells for five dollars a copy, and get him invited to a lot of ministers' conferences as the headline speaker. But unless he loves men and wants to communicate the gospel to them he will never be a real servant of the Word. He will be only a stuffed shirt of the Word.

A man cannot commute from study to pulpit and back again, looking at life only through the glass of his moving train, and have any real notion of how the gospel must be proclaimed. As Seward Hiltner has emphasized, "One cannot say, 'I have a

[3]Harry Emerson Fosdick, "What Is the Matter with Preaching?," *Harper's Magazine*, CLVII (July, 1928), 135.

single secure way of testifying to my faith on all occasions and do not have to take into account the relativities of human need.' Instead, testimony to Christian faith is always a compound of the eternal gospel and specific need." [4] The preacher who really cares for his message will care for how it is heard, for what it means when it strikes the magic tympanum of the listener's ear.

For my own part, I like the picture we have of Stephen Leacock, the famous Canadian economist and humorist, the time he was at a party with friends and was asked to come to a local radio station for an impromptu broadcast: he refused to go unless he could take his friends into the studio with him, saying that his humor was for people and that he could not be humorous in an empty room with a microphone. That is the way it ought to be for preaching, and involvement in an adequately conceived program of pastoral care is one guarantee that it will be so.

A corollary of these remarks is that real pastoral concern inevitably makes preaching more dialogical. It not only makes sermons more human, it makes them more responsive to the particular thoughts and reactions of the specific persons in the congregation. In other words, the attitude of pastoral care assists the minister in making the preaching of the Word a cooperative affair in which the laity bear part of the responsibility for what is actually said in the sermon. Dietrich Ritschl, in his little book *A Theology of Proclamation,* even suggests that the laymen ought to have planning sessions with the clergy in which they help to choose the sermon texts and come to general agreement on the interpretation of them. Such a program, if followed consistently, would certainly enhance the laity's feeling of stewardship for the gospel and develop a sounder approach to local Christian education.

But whether we go this far or not, we ought at least to be aware of the fact that the man in the pew does talk back to the preacher. Maybe he doesn't do it out loud in the minister's

⁴Seward Hiltner, *The Christian Shepherd* (Nashville, Abingdon Press, 1959), p. 17.

presence, but you may be sure he does it under his breath or in the privacy of his home or club. Reuel Howe, Director of the Institute for Advanced Pastoral Studies, has tried to turn this *sotto voce* criticism into creative possibilities by experimenting with what he calls "sermon backfire sessions," in which small groups discuss the pastor's latest sermon. Howe deems it best for the preacher himself not to be present at such sessions, lest he tend to inhibit the critics from giving free voice to their true feelings about the sermon; he may take advantage of the critique by hearing it all later on a tape recording. The curative effects of such sessions, as I can testify from having talked with students about the tapes provided for them by lay critics in churches where they have preached, are often amazing. At the very least, they make the preacher aware that the sermon must come to grips with the real problems people face, and not, as Edgar Jackson has put it, merely "scratch where they don't itch."

Of course a man cannot preach dialogical sermons if he cannot listen to what others are saying, if his gospel has become monologic and he has lost his hearing. A friend of mine was once working on a book on communication (I don't know if he ever finished it) in which one chapter was to be entitled "Communication as Listening." What an important aspect of communication it is! How much more effective our preaching would be if it only proceeded out of the combined results of our listening to the Word of God and listening—really listening—to the hearts of men. Another friend of mine has a minister acquaintance who always writes his sermons with a particular lawyer in his congregation in mind; every phrase and idea is tested against what the minister thinks the reaction of that lawyer will be. That is not a bad way to write out sermons, if only one does not forget that the whole world is not made up of lawyers, that there are secretaries and athletes and plumbers and freckle-faced little girls, too, and that they must hear the gospel so that it means something to them.

Another way in which pastoral care makes a contribution to preaching is in influencing the sermon to be more permissive in tone and outlook. Not that the sermon should be spineless, like the jellyfish, and do nothing so much as seem inoffensive to everybody; there is a natural offense to the most faithful preaching of the gospel, an offense that ends by humbling us and bringing us to repentance. But there is a difference between the offensiveness of the gospel and the offensiveness of the preacher. The gospel offends by the directness with which it brings the love of God within the flimsy curtains of the sinner's life. But it is not the minister's business to follow it in and gape at the sinner's nakedness. He, of all men, should have a depth of understanding and a breadth of experience that will enable him to speak of the grace of God without sounding like a hanging judge; on the contrary, his voice should come to men with the promise of rescue, the hope of redemption. The sermon ought always to constitute a pre-counseling situation, and prepare the way for the most effective personal confrontation between the minister and the counselee. It should set up a relation of confidence between the clergyman and the person in the pew, so that the person in the pew realizes he may approach the clergyman about any problem, however delicate or distasteful, and find reflected in him the same kind of magnanimity and graciousness of spirit as that characterizing the gospel he proclaims.

All of this, of course, puts a necessary emphasis on the healthiness of the minister himself. What sort of person is he? Has he really experienced the grace of God in his own life? Has grace expanded and filled out the contours of his personality? Is his house in good order? These things come through in a man's preaching, not just in what he says but in every nuance of his bearing, his gestures, his inflections, in the very tone of his voice. Have you ever noticed what wonderful persons the best psychiatrists seem to be? How warm and strong and generous they are? Doesn't this say something to the preacher about the way he communicates his gospel? It has a lot to do with the kind of response we are able to generate in those to whom we preach. If we are hurried and harried, then we will hurry and harry the congregation. A nervous person will be agitated by the sermon.

If we are uncertain and insecure in our private lives, then this will reveal itself in our preaching, and those who are uncertain and insecure will only be convinced that the rest of the world is in as bad a shape as they are. If we are strict in the letter of the law and narrow in our view of man, we cannot keep it out of the sermon, try as we will, and men will fear to open to us the secrets of their pasts or the gateways to their present enigmas and imbroglios. Phillips Brooks was right when he said that preaching is truth through personality, and the personality is as important in the communication of the gospel as the truth itself is. In fact, truth is never separable from personality. We stamp the gospel with something of ourselves when we preach it.

Another way by which pastoral care supports the task of preaching is in the constant encouragement it gives the preacher to see the working out of the gospel in men's lives. If a man were never able to descend from the pulpit and follow his people home, up flights of tenement stairs or down some rural path, even if he had them tenderly in mind when he composed his sermons, he could not help becoming apathetic and wondering whether there were really any use in his preaching at all. It is in seeing the reaction to the gospel, in viewing the way Christ makes mastery of a man's life, that we are enheartened and enlivened for a creative ministry, and that we are willing, even when there is so much against the gospel, to dare all for its sake and the sake of the people. Nothing else so rescues us from the deadly routinizing of our various duties. Nothing else so fires us on, week after week, to find new ways of putting the gospel, of setting it forth to do its work.

Enough has been said, I think, to indicate the significance of pastoral care to the ministry of the pulpit. There is no doubt of that significance.

But now let us turn the page over and read on the other side the importance of preaching to the ministry of pastoral care, and why preaching is and must be central to the work of personal counseling. It is summed up in a single sentence: *The preaching of the Word of God, and that preaching alone, is*

*able to prevent the diffuseness and secularity by which counsel-
ing is frequently victimized, and return the matter of pastoral
care in upon the Word and sacrament, which are always central
in the forming of the Christian community.*

Wherever there is not felt a strong sense of mission for the
proclaiming of the Word, the ministry of pastoral care tends to
become eclectic, appealing only to those concepts and teachings
of the church which appear to reinforce its own theories, and
even at times adulterating those concepts and teachings in order
to make them seem synonymous with its theories. Forgiveness,
for example, is a key word in both preaching and counseling,
but it does not mean precisely the same thing to the preacher
and counselor. To the preacher it sums up the many-faceted
redemptive activity of God and the whole matter of man's acceptance by the Divine; it means atonement through Christ
and restoration to a Father whose care for his children is infinite
and unsearchable. But to the counselor it often means, first of all,
self-acceptance, and then, if it ever means anything else, acceptance by others, and finally, though the chances of reaching this
stage have diminished considerably, acceptance by God or whatever principle stands in his place. In other words, there is a
secularization of the doctrine of forgiveness, accomplished by
reversing the normal pattern in the Christian faith, wherein
acceptance by God (announced first) leads to acceptance of
others and finally to the acceptance of the self. I emphasize that
this is not always the case in the counseling relationship; the
counselor who has been trained in theological approach as well
as in the psychological dimensions of his vocation is usually well
aware of the dangerous subjectivity introduced into the counseling process by the reversal of the traditional pattern. But the
reversal occurs frequently enough to mark it as a tendency among
counselors who are not preachers.

Frederic Wood has noted the danger even to the Christian
counselor that he will fail to make clear to the counselee that he
is not himself the source of forgiveness, but that the forgiveness
of which he speaks is a forgiveness he has himself received from

God and now points the counselee toward. "Some pastors," says Wood, "feel that the very fact that they are identified as religious practitioners relieves them of having to provide any explicit Christian orientation to their pastoral care. But this smacks suspiciously of an attempt to let a clerical collar or a church building do that which only a living person can do, proclaim the presence of the living Christ in our lives." [5]

Out of the positiveness of our own experience of forgiveness, and that alone, are we able to refuse to be the God the counselee is looking for and to give him the kind of "cheap grace" he is begging for. And it is the periodic proclamation of the Word in public that keeps us on course, that reminds us that ours is a useful gospel because it is transcendent and is not manipulable to our minor schemes and purposes, because it is God's own gospel of forgiveness.

Thurneysen says that the man who comes to us for help is really unaware of sin as the total fact which entirely imprisons him and that he does not really long for the forgiving Word as the only effective remedy. What he really hopes is that the resources for answering his problem are inside of him. He wants us to believe in him and in those resources within him, and to say something that will help him to regroup and seize the mastery of the situation again. He may even be willing to make great personal sacrifices in order to achieve this. But in the end it is a way without grace and without God that he wants; in his indomitable human pride, he stubbornly refuses to surrender himself completely to the God who is other than he, who transcends him and his situation and his secret desires.

"It is all-important that we do not give in," advises Thurneysen, "but rather block this road for him." We must block it even at the price of disappointing and offending him. Of course we shall exert every effort to understand his problem from a human point of view, and to stand with him under the weight of his situation. And we shall bring into play every principle and resource of psychology that we can. But our counseling is not

[5] Wood, *op. cit.*, pp. 128-129.

merely psychological and must not pretend to be. We represent God, the church, prayer, the Scriptures; and at one point in the conversation there must come a breach in which we introduce these matters into the conversation, in which we do everything possible to transfer the counselee's concerns from the human and psychological realm into the quite different realm disclosed by the Word of God. How we do this is another matter; but that it be done is indispensable. "It will determine the worth or worthlessness of our pastoral care. We must be perfectly clear that if we evade this breach, we deviate from our line, be it only by a hair's breadth. If we join the counselee—perhaps only tentatively and experimentally—on the ground from which he first comes, we base our pastoral care not on the Word but on a secular understanding of man and on a corresponding 'natural theology.' We may subsequently, perhaps very searchingly and earnestly, speak of sin and grace and Jesus Christ—even the anthroposophists also speak of them!—but fundamentally, our efforts will be lost, for our partner in conversation will fill all our words, even the highest and last words of faith, with a mystic or moralistic or philosophical content dissolving them from within. From his point of departure he cannot do otherwise. But he will not really be able to hear that his sins are forgiven in Jesus Christ."[6]

There is the great danger, that we run in a substitute gospel and do not really connect the counselee with the community of faith where men live in the knowledge of absolute forgiveness. The individual is not rescued at all from his isolation and the church is not built up. The gospel has been diluted. Forgiveness has become such a thin and watery gruel that it is really only a pseudo-forgiveness, with no power to reorient life or sustain it thereafter.

But now let us be more positive, and see how pastoral care works when it is properly grounded in the ministry of the Word of God, when it takes its inception from the act of proclamation in the gathered church.

The sermon is the moment of encounter. The minister has read

[6] Thurneysen, op. cit., p. 92.

from the Scriptures, and stands behind the pulpit to declare, "This day is the Scripture fulfilled in your hearing." He speaks an old message in fresh accents and contemporary idioms. It is plain that he is talking to every man's deepest needs, yet without personally offending anyone or seeming to accuse any individual. He sets forth the Word, clothed in the best human words, and applies it to emergent occasions in the lives of the congregation. Persons who came to the service grieved by finite circumstances, perhaps even without realizing that they were so grieved, prick up their ears at any word suggesting understanding of their situations, and are a ready field for the planting of some eternal seed. They hale the tenderest sympathy, however general, and know it could be meant for them. They resolve to pursue it further, to see if the bearer of this Word has not something in reserve for them alone, something he could not deliver in the presence of the general congregation but would be willing, under importunity, to divulge in the privacy of the counsel chamber. A word is exchanged at the door, a telephone call is made, an invitation is extended—by some sign, what can be done in private is begun.

Nor does it end there for the preaching! Week by week, the preaching becomes food for thought, provocation to inquiry and to grace, and helps to bear along the entire business of the counseling. The minister discovers new life in the personal contact, and preaches with new enthusiasm at seeing Christ made real in the explorations of the counselee. His new life, shared, means more new life for the counselee. And on and on it goes, multiplied by the number of people with whom it is happening.

And it is not only with those who come to church with problems that something happens. There is another significant aspect to what occurs when the Word is preached, and that is that it starts something creative in people who did not have any specific problems, or did not think that they did. As psychiatrist Rollo May has demonstrated, "Creativity occurs in an act of encounter, and is to be understood with this encounter as its center."[7] Cre-

---

[7] Rollo May, "Creativity and Encounter," *Union Seminary Quarterly Review*, XVIII, No. 4 (May, 1963), 369.

ativity, that is, is not solely the result of something inside a
person, but of the impingement of something on the consciousness
from outside, producing anxiety or challenge and causing the
response of creativeness. And this happens in preaching. The
individual is confronted with the gospel, and hears it in a way
he has never heard it before. Something begins to happen to
him. Maybe the whole sea-shelf of his life gives way and there is
a cataclysmic upheaval in him. He suddenly becomes a candidate
for a counseling session. He had no idea that he needed anything.
But now he finds himself a child in the forest again, and must
have help. This time he must find his true self, and pastoral
counseling can assist him in doing it. The public preaching of the
Word has produced a crisis which will now be met and worked
out privately.

This is the real interdependence of preaching and pastoral
care. Preaching announces the gospel and in that moment ushers
in the New Order of God and his Christ; and pastoral care works
for the securing of that Order once it has been introduced.
Neither can be completely effective apart from the other.

Here is an illustration that may suggest something of the way
in which they work together. One spring a few years ago there
was an unusually heavy rainfall in the lower Appalachians, producing ravaging floodwaters in the small-creek country of West
Virginia and eastern Kentucky. Many towns were inundated or
cut off from the outside world. Water supplies were contaminated
and floodstuffs were scarce. Rescue workers labored around the
clock, poling small boats up and down city streets to relieve dis-
tressed and helpless citizens. When the waters had finally abated
and the teams from relief agencies were able to go into the areas
with sorely needed supplies and assistance, the method of operation in numerous communities was this: The townspeople were
called together at some central location and an explanation was
made of the way in which the workers would assist them. If
supplies were to be rationed, the people were told how to register
for them, and then the workers began rolling up their sleeves
and moved out into various parts of town and went to work.

The process in the church is not unsimilar. The people assemble for the preaching of the Word. There is therefore some sense of community, of being involved in things together, of sharing responsibilities and resources. The Word is a word of help, of deliverance. But what takes place in the assembly is mainly the announcement. From there, the matter must be pursued into the private lives of the congregation, down this street and that, in this home and that, until what was promised in the public meeting has been fulfilled in terms of every man's personal existence. And in preaching and pastoral care there is always the weekly return to the assembly in order that difficulties may be observed and progress registered, and that, having hitched up again, the process may go on.

In my own experience, I have never known any man to carry his pastoral ministry successfully into the lives of many persons who did not at one time or another sit under his preaching; and I have known few men who preached successfully in the pulpit and then were not able to minister personally to the persons who heard them. I knew two ministers who occupied the same pastorate in sequence. The first busied himself with going from house to house, conducting his ministry on an intimate and personal basis, and letting his preaching pretty much fare for itself, taking the leftovers of his time and energy; and he said, "My people are healthy and we have a fine relationship." The man who followed him was a great preacher in the true sense of the word. He fenced the hours of his preparation, and when he mounted the pulpit it was almost always with an important thing to say, said in a way that made it catch like a burr in the souls of the people. He was not in that pastorate six months before he found himself virtually surrounded by sick and desperate persons, with men coming at all hours to confess their secret needs and fears. Need I say that the congregation had not changed since the first man's ministry? The first man was a good man, but he had just not discovered the real heart of his ministry. He was plying the periphery when he should have been tending to the center of things. No man should surrender the multiple phases of his ministry in order to preach, but if he does not preach, he might just as well give them up.

"The two parts of a preacher's work are always in rivalry," said Phillips Brooks in his *Lectures on Preaching*. "When you find that you can never sit down to study and write without the faces of the people, who you know need your care, looking out at you from the paper; and yet you never can go out among your people without hearing your forsaken study reproaching you and calling you home, you may easily come to believe that it would be good indeed if you could be one or other of two things, and not both; either a preacher or a pastor, but not the two together. But I assure you you are wrong. The two things are not two, but one. There may be preachers here and there with such a deep, intense insight into the general humanity, that they can speak to men without knowing the men to whom they speak. Such preachers are very rare; and other preachers, who have not their power, trying to do it, are sure to preach to some unreal, unhuman man of their own imagination. There are some pastors here and there with such a constantly lofty and spiritual view of little things, that they can go about from house to house, year after year, and deal with men and women at their common work, and lift the men and women to themselves, and never fall to the level of the men and women whom they teach. Such pastors are rare; and other men, trying to do it, and never in more formal way from the pulpit treating truth in its larger aspects, are sure to grow frivolous gossips or tiresome machines. The preacher needs to be pastor, that he may preach to real men. The pastor must be preacher, that he may keep the dignity of his work alive. The preacher, who is not a pastor, grows remote. The pastor, who is not a preacher, grows petty. Never be content to let men truthfully say of you, 'He is a preacher, but no pastor'; or, 'He is a pastor, but no preacher.' Be both; for you cannot really be one unless you also are the other."

4

PREACHING AND CHRISTIAN EDUCATION

If the minister of the average urban or suburban church today had only his twenty-minute sermon slot as his and the church's contact with the members of the congregation, how utterly hopeless his task would seem. Imagine five hundred parishioners of all shapes and sizes, income and educational brackets, social and professional backgrounds, descending on a spot of perhaps one thousand square feet—a bawling, crawling, sprawling (and, in the South, drawling) lump of humanity—for one hour of hymn-singing, prayers, and preaching each week; and then not necessarily the *same* five hundred every time. If the sermon were not part of a larger program, part of a conspiracy to save the parishioners from unreflective and unredemptive living, it would indeed be futile. "Thirty minutes to wake the dead," John Ruskin called it. And now only twenty, or maybe fifteen, and that in the face of such overwhelming odds. Maybe the dead could be stirred, momentarily, but not awakened.

The problem is especially difficult today because of the increasing secularization of life. (Not that secularization is an unhealthy trend; on the contrary, it is a symptom of revitalization and expansion, of discovery and new awareness, and only the

72

most reactionary Christian will actually deplore it and cringe in the face of it.) Life is no longer neat and orderly for those who attend church. The church may still represent the significant center or nucleus of their existence (they must believe it; why else do they continue to come?), but that nucleus is much smaller than it once was. The proportion of their knowledge and experience lying on the periphery or even beyond the periphery of that nucleus is far larger than was ever true before. Therefore they have a greater sense of freedom from the church, and with it a corresponding anxiety about responsibility. They are more existentialist than any people before them; in a large measure, they choose who they will be and how they will live their lives. Civilization has become a pluralistic wilderness.

"We find ourselves in an exodus-culture," says Johannes Hoekendijk, "and exodus will remain the order of the day."[1] Christians are no longer settled and sure. Like everyone else in the twentieth century, they are searching for patterns of meaning. They are no longer content with beliefs learned out of a catechism; they know that the only beliefs that are soul-size for them are the ones they have tried on and know to have relevance in their lives. As Hoekendijk observes, a characteristic phenomenon of our time is described by the word *Dauerreflektion,* which "refers to the attitude of being continually on the way in our thinking, always again questioning, without necessarily seeking a point of rest or a terminal point for our thinking in a definite answer."

Church-attenders today are intelligent, eclectic, wary, increasingly independent, and restless—and no preacher is able to meet their needs more than partially in the Sunday morning sermon.

How vastly important, then, has become the teaching ministry of the church, a ministry shared by competent and dedicated lay men and women who in effect form a variegated network of instruction and experimentation and counseling in support of the preaching and appropriation of the gospel. As one minister re-

---

[1] Johannes Hoekendijk, *The Church Inside Out* (Philadelphia: Westminster, 1964), p. 79.

cently said at a dinner honoring the faculty and staff of his church school and its related programs, "Whenever I get to feeling, like Elijah, that I am all alone in the work, I remember these joyful and indefatigable comrades; and psychologically, as well as in other ways, they mean much more to me than Elijah's brothers-at-arms, because they are known to me individually and personally."

It is not that teaching was not regarded as an important aspect of the church's ministry in earlier generations; certainly it was much emphasized during the first two or three centuries of the church's life and during the period of the Reformation, when the desire for religious instruction led to the founding of school systems and universities throughout the Western world. The growth of the church school or Sunday school system since its inauguration by Robert Raikes in 1780 has been little short of phenomenal. But the church has never been faced by the technological crisis before, and has probably never before experienced the kind of cultural saturation that confronts it today. The dimensions of the knowledge explosion, astronomically hiked by television (for the first time in history, says McLuhan, people travel around the world to see what they have already seen, and to judge it by the image they have received on the screen in their own den or living room), have become staggering, and have precipitated a crisis in the church's ministry and its self-understanding of that ministry—a crisis that cannot be met by merely traditional educational approaches and equipment. It is a time for the greatest teaching that has ever been done, and for the most sensitive teaching that has ever been done.

Now that civilization has, in its Spenglerian western movement, reached around and seized its own tail, girdling the globe, and has therefore begun to become impacted, man requires much more than a frontier faith. The simple abecedarian approach to salvation is no longer sufficient. That mythical figure the average man has much more time and education today with which to consider the subleties and intricacies of belief, and the old evangelicalism that was predicated on a Ptolemaic world structure and a Calvinistic adherence to Scripture, while it may linger temporarily in the unconscious, or even in the conscious, as a relic of the good old days of religion, is really woefully inadequate to him as an explanation of the way things are in his life.

The way that this fact is beginning to come home particularly to younger Christians is illustrated in an anecdote which I believe was first told by Professor Kenneth Chafin. A veteran "soul-winner" (a phenomenon known principally in right-wing American Protestantism), who made a habit of backing people into corners by his knowledge of the Scriptures and then shanghaiing them into the Kingdom of God, was being accompanied during an afternoon of housecalls by an expectant novice in the soul-winning business. Again and again the novice stood by as his experienced elder partner adroitly maneuvered his "marks" into the corner where he wanted them and then continued to badger them until they had emitted their cries of surrender.

Late in the afternoon, the two men drove to an address in an elegant suburb, parked the car, and walked across a velvety carpet of grass to the front door. As they passed the picture window, they paused to glance inside. The occupant of the house was relaxing in his skivvies, having a can of beer. He was sitting in one of those big leather massage chairs, tilted back at an angle almost to the horizontal, and was sleepily sighting along his big toe to the color television set across the room. A handsome Dalmatian dog lay beside the chair, and the man languorously stroked its head from time to time. The young soul-winner turned to the older man as his finger was on the bell and blurted out his secret thought: "What kind of good news do we have for *him?*"

It was a proper question. What kind of good news do we have for men in the affluent society? If the God of crisis-theology is primarily a God "of the gaps," of the yawning abysses in the socio-economic structure where men are made most drastically aware of their finitude and dependence on some inscrutable force beyond their own powers of comprehension, then crisis-theology is hardly the most suitable vehicle for the gospel in an age that is hellbent on narrowing the gaps and closing up the fissures. As Dietrich Bonhoeffer suggested from his prison cell, perhaps we have got to quit thinking of God as inhabiting the edges of life and think of him as living at the center. That may betray us into a kind of Christian pantheism we are dead scared of, but we are always being betrayed into something or other by the times we live in, and we do well to admit it. At least it is obvious that our old understanding of evangelism as a Scripture-citing, logic-begging, proof-texting religious legerdemain is as foolish and futile as it is out of date. We are finally forced, four hundred years late, to a more sacramental and less narrowistic view of the universe, and, like Francis Bacon, to take all knowl-edge, psychological and sociological as well as theological and soteriological, to be our province.

The sermon is (if it is good) an act of confrontation. It does pose a crisis, even when it is post-Barthian, post-Brunnerian, post-crisis-theology. The gospel even as good news, as identifier of mystery and presence in the world, becomes judgment to the man who has not seen the mystery and presence and has camped out all his life unaware of being on the edge of them. Thwump! A sermon on "The Secularity of Grace" makes a big puckering pockmark right in the middle of a man's middle-aged, middle-class composure, leaves him sucking in air like a pump with its feeder hose out of water, and he wonders why he doesn't just cave in from the pressures and become as flat and two-dimen-sional as he realizes his existence has been, when he had eyes to see but did not see and ears to hear but did not hear.

This happens in preaching, just as effectively as it did when a skinny New Englander named Jonathan Edwards was sublimat-ing his sadistic instincts by dangling parishioners over the bromide fumes of a linguistic and rhetorical hell. A lot of the terminology in the psychology of conversion has been changed, but the ex-perience has not been greatly altered. There are still the char-acteristics of dramatic enlightenment, deep and sometimes re-morseful repentance, catharsis or cleansing, and the feeling of renewal and the recovery of hope.

But we are in a position now to understand better than we ever have that men are not edified, not built up, merely by the repetition of the confrontation experience. This is the mistake of most evangelical worship: it takes for granted the necessity of reconstituting at every occasion, including the Sunday morning hour for the gathered congregation, the marks and flavor of the initial conversion hour, so that the tent-meeting aura is gradually taken to be the normative one for every kind of spiritual event. Confrontation must give way to what is more than confrontation. It must give way to growth, to elaboration, to expansion, to qualification and analysis, to identification with the life process and the social environment, to questions and absorption, to self-understanding and meaning and devotion. Otherwise it arrests the development of personality instead of freeing it, snags it at a moment in time and at a particular configuration of emotional factors out of an infinite range and variety of factors, hangs it up on the end of the very diving board on the way to emancipation and development.

The tragedy of Christian education in previous generations has lain in its anxiety to reproduce its own kind, to indoctrinate and dogmatize and anesthetize and sterilize, so much so that, irony of ironies, it has been known to repudiate its own offspring, secular education, for encouraging openness and receptivity to new ideas and information. And now it is paying the price by finding itself substandard, banal and uninformed in the face of modern knowledgeability and sophistication. Only in recent years, with the advent of new curricula like those of the United Presbyterian Church and certain innovative and privateering churches which have written their own literature, have we begun to close the disastrous gap between standardized church school materials and the much more exciting levels of secular education.

As one critic told a conference on Christian education, most church schools have been organized around a world view that was outmoded a century ago.[2] Man has changed, and his un-

---

[2] "Bye-Bye, Sunday School," *The Christian Century*, August 16, 1967, pp. 1038-1039.

derstanding of reality has changed. He no longer sees his nature as fixed, determined, inflexible. He no longer believes that the existing patterns are unchangeable. And he no longer believes that he must listen to external religious authorities, for they are just as suspect in his book as political and social authorities. The job of religious education, said the critic, is to help liberate this man from his religious past as well as his political and sociological past.

This, it seems to me, is a much healthier viewpoint than that generally expressed by religious educators in the past. To borrow Jonathan Swift's analogy, we have too long spun our entire educational programs out of our own entrails, like the spider, and it is time we began moving out over God's creation like the honeybee.

The major confrontation experience of the church will continue to be in the hour of worship and in the occasion of the preaching of the Word. There is something about the congregation of believers, assembling for the highest moments together, that mysteriously produces the conditions which favor the most poetic and myth-weaving statements of the gospel. But the confrontation must necessarily be prolonged and extended into the life of the church through the educational process. The church school and its affiliated programs become the workshop in which the declarations of the plenary session are pursued, examined, analyzed, debated, tested, assimilated. Confrontation necessarily goes on there too, for any new fact, any new idea, can become critical in a man's life, but the primary task of education is one of expansion, definition, query and criticism.

Even the counseling responsibilities arising from the act of proclamation find their extension into the educational areas of the church. The redevelopment or reorientation of human life requires a concomitant program of reeducation; responses and reactions based on previously held world views must be rethought and redirected; new emphases must be discovered and solidified by the acquisition of new knowledge or the rearrangement of old. Some very good teachers spend much of their spare time listening to the problems of class members and helping to elicit in the members' thinking beliefs and ideas capable of supporting significant changes occurring in their lives. They are aware that life is really a process, a dynamic, ever-forming thing, and not a fixed and unalterable pattern at all. Instead of supporting the status quo, they are always seizing the advantage in any situation to test men's substructures, their faulty underriggings, and precipitate crisis in their lives, for they know that growth is occasioned by crises, especially if there is sympathetic and capable guidance in the times of particular stress. Teachers with this approach to their tasks thus become undershepherds in the church, aiding the work of the minister and extending the power of the gospel that is preached from the pulpit.

I remember one church whose inner understanding of its task as a church impressed me very much. There were three full-time ministers in the church, but none of them was designated "senior minister" or "executive pastor" or anything like that. They performed certain functions according to their abilities, but they were aware of the cooperativeness of their venture. And they were constantly reminding their parishioners that they, the people of God, were really shepherds and pastors to each other and to the community. Consequently the parishioners were extremely active in caring for the unfortunate, the poor, the bereaved, the uneducated, the elderly, the displaced and the dispossessed in their city. They operated a medical mission in the ghetto area of town, ran a day nursery for working mothers, sponsored innumerable short- and long-term projects in behalf of people who had no previous interest in the church at all. They were the most vital congregation of believers and workers I think I have ever seen.

All of this activity was supported by a creative and responsive educational program. The church maintained a three-year "College of Christian Life" for all new members—and found that most of the graduates stayed on either as teachers or as eager students. There were sensitive and extremely contemporary courses in biblical literature, theology, ethics, and Christian history. Traditional understandings of these subjects provided the staple element in the classes, but discussion was freewheeling and wide-ranging, never resting in tradition because it was tradition, always pushing on and beyond old horizons to new configurations of belief and understanding. The people had discovered that there is nothing stale about the Christian faith, only about the way some persons regard it and deal with it. They were excited, zestful, and happy, because they felt themselves stretching and growing all the time.

What about the preaching in such a dynamic situation? Did it prove to be superfluous, something that could be abandoned because of the universal alertness of the congregation? Not for a minute! The pulpit proved to be the very natural center for all of the activity and engagement of the people. They listened, were moved, and went out to work (they reminded me of Frederick Wenz's definition of Christians as people who come together like paratroopers for a briefing on Sunday before being dropped behind enemy lines on Monday); then they came back again eager to hear some more, eager to be moved again, eager to go out that way again. The rhythm was that of systole and diastole, contracttion and expansion, for the proclamation of the gospel was the heart of the entire program. It breathed life into the educational task and into the total ministry of the church, and these in turn brought to the preaching courage and imagination and sustenance to be what it so emphatically was.

What do we say then about the relationship of preaching and Christian education? It is much more intimate than often meets the eye. C. H. Dodd performed a notable service in *The Apostolic Preaching* by separating for us the strands of kerygma and didache, or preaching and teaching, in the early church. We are able to speak much more certainly of the respective functions of the two acts than we were previously. But Professor John Knox is right to remind us (in *The Integrity of Preaching*) that they are not easily separable and that we must not be unmindful of their interdependence. A good sermon is a prime teaching device at the same time that it is proclamation; and a good lesson inevitably ends by making the gospel more real and visible in the lives of the students.

The minister who is perceptive of this sensitive interdependence will consciously foster an interplay and creative tension between the two. His sermons will continually prod men to the desire for Christian growth and nurture by provoking their interest on various topics, by confronting them with the immensities of the faith, by arousing them to questions on contemporary ethical practice, by challenging them every time to keep moving on, to keep digging deeper, in their understanding of the gospel and its ways of finding fulfillment in their lives and times. As a result, study groups should be constantly spinning off and growing out of the ferment of good preaching. And these should in turn have their effect upon the preaching—probing it, rebutting it, reveling in it, expanding on it—so that the two go round together like the gingham dog and the calico cat, increasing the circumferences of meaning and existence at the heart of the Christian community.

I have in mind another church where this reciprocal relationship exists, where the pastor through serious homiletical work is consistently stretching the minds and hearts of his people for true discipleship, and the people in turn are responding with the highest that is in them, studying to be sensitive to the subtler outlines of grace and the softer whispers of Christian duty and vocation, so that the preaching Sunday by Sunday enters ears better and better attuned to discover its nuances as well as its central thrust. That pastor has turned down invitation after invitation from larger and more affluent churches to accept their pulpits because he could not bear to leave the stimulus where he is, for he would be a fish out of water, a crab out of sand, a plant out of earth; and the members of his church cannot bear the thoughts of moving away or otherwise being taken out of the fellowship, for they have discovered there a dimension of Christian life and growth they never dreamed existed. Moreover, the church is performing a major witness in the larger community as these excited and exciting Christians bear testimony in the schools and offices and factories and stores to what dynamic faith really is.

Because of the interplay between sermon and education, the serious minister will find it rewarding occasionally to preach on the texts employed in the lessons of the church school. There are several advantages to this. If the minister is not accustomed to preaching by the method of *lectio continua* as provided for by the lectionaries of the liturgical churches, then following the International Sunday School Lessons or a similar plan offers a corrective to what someone has called "round-the-year butterfly preaching," which alights now here, now there. It also provides the congregation with a sense of ecumenicity, of being part of the wider household of faith, because it gives them a specific continuity with other churches whose interest is focused on the same text on a given Sunday. But most important, preaching on the text of the church school lesson means that the minister may take advantage of a prepared situation, of greater anticipation and concentration on the part of the congregation. Karl Barth spoke in *The Word of God and the Word of Man* of the strategic significance to preaching of the mood of anticipation and excitement among the people—"an expectancy that something great, crucial, and even momentous is to happen." No sermon ever achieves so much when the people are brought to it cold as it does when they arrive with preparation on their parts to hear what the preacher, out of the depths of his own prayer and imagination, will bring forth on the text or subject at hand.

All of this presupposes that there will be a certain freshness and vivacity to what the minister says about the text, and that he will not merely deliver up the hash and rehash of the meal that has already been devoured. With his intimate knowledge of the Scriptures and his more thorough acquaintance with human life, he ought to be able, if he is not a lazy or indifferent fellow, to marshal the materials of the case in such a helpful and compelling way as to clinch for everyone the intentionality and meaning of the text, and so give life among his people to the ageless Word so willing to revisit the haunts of men.

Some churches include among their educational projects experimentation in theater and dance and art. Judson Memorial Church in New York City sponsors poetry readings and liturgical dance in its sanctuary worship. The American Church in Paris provides a theater hall with a professional production group to stage contemporary dramas, and a Wednesday-Friday night festival of poetry reading, folk-singing, and amateur theatricals for college students. And the preaching in these churches picks up, mirrors, elongates and debates with the viewpoints of secular life thus imported into the church by keen modern minds. The effect can be exhilarating. Christians soon get the idea that ghetto religion is not enough, that the world, not the sanctuary, is their arena. They understand what Hoekendijk meant when he said that the order of revelation is not God-church-world but God-world-church. The gospel becomes more real to them and they become more real to the gospel.

It is sometimes said complainingly that there is not enough gospel in Christian education, especially in the more daringly secular edges of it such as those mentioned above. But a genuine closeness between preaching and teaching in the church can almost guarantee the existence of a proper content at the heart of Christian education. It keeps the kerygmatic framework, the evangelical vision, at the center of things, and thus helps to prevent a fatal diffusion of interest into the more historical or legal or literary aspects of what is being taught.

D. Campbell Wyckoff has effectively contended, in *The Gospel and Christian Education,* that only the thoughtful ministering of the gospel is sufficient to be considered as the central principle of Christian education. Other things have been central at various times in the church's life: the Bible, doctrinal formulations, sundry theologies, even the church itself. But only the gospel, says Wyckoff, is both general enough and specific enough to be an adequate principle. It guarantees the importance of biblical study, but offers at the same time the assurance of a contemporary sensibility to that study. It provides doctrinal and theological considerations and conclusions, but never at the expense of life or spirit. It brings the church into being, but is never caught in the cultural net that so easily entangles the church. The central aim of the gospel is always to form Christ more fully in persons. And if the gospel is primary in Christian education, then it will determine in large measure the curricular and organizational forms which that education should take.

Thus good preaching performs its seminal service to the education of the church; nothing helps more to keep the gospel alive and strongly defined in the educational process. Though by the same token, of course, nothing does more than poor preaching, or preaching that does not see itself clearly as a proclamatory act making God's presence more "realizable" in human affairs, to smother and extinguish the proper breathing of the gospel in the whole body of the church. With practice, you get so you can feel what a church is like by almost any kind of sustained or substantive contact with it. You enter a Sunday school class and you know from the discussion whether the preacher is good or mediocre. You look at the library, if it has one (that in itself says something), and you can tell how provocative and challenging a man he is. You attend a meeting of the main committee of the church, and you soon sense how it is with the pulpit. Anywhere in the life of the church you can see what is going on in the preaching, for the preaching is the heart of the matter, and it more than anything else vitalizes or stifles the rest of the enterprise.

It is amazing, when one thinks about it, how a wise and consistent intimacy between preaching and teaching will serve to keep a sense of mystery alive in the business of teaching, a sense it so often wants in churches today. Why is it so difficult, so incredibly difficult, to find stimulating and competent laymen willing to devote themselves to the important work of leading discussion groups and teaching church school classes? May not one reason be that teaching is ordinarily considered a very prosaic task, one without either the challenge or the rewards of preaching, that it is at best a hard job and at worst a very dull one? Many churches have done much to foster such an opinion by their half-hearted and indecently slipshod approach to Christian education. Every time they have settled for merely a smooth-running organization, with enough teachers or teacher-figures to supply all the classes and keep all the records but without any real concern for precision and imagination and growth, they have succeeded only in lowering the dignity and worth of true teaching in the eyes of the entire parish.

By leading us into a more sensitive awareness of the mysteries of God and of the faith (the Christian faith is not some little pond you can walk around in thirty minutes, said A. J. Gossip, and then say of it, "There, that is that"), preaching can restore to us the idea that something mysterious transpires in the class-room too, that men's lives are changed in dialogical and cate-chetical situations as well as in proclamatory ones, and that God is performing the work of conversion and redemption under the efforts of the teacher just as he does it under the preaching of the minister. So many teachers have been taught to have only a dry, unreflective attitude toward the textual substance of their les-sons. They miss the romance, the excitement, the magic, of teaching. They fulfill their obligations mechanically and never discover the fourth dimension of what they are doing. Conse-quently, they must be forever coddled and encouraged to con-tinue in their work, urged to put one foot in front of the other, week after week, year after year, considering their secret em-barrassment over such a poor job and the necessity of going on a part of their inescapable Christian duty and self-flagellation. It is this plodding, mechanical attitude that has misled most of our congregations into their present low opinion of the educational ministry of the church. If they could only once see genuine Chris-tian teaching at work, see it and feel its exciting effects, there would be no shortage of workers and teachers; the churches would produce them spontaneously and naturally, as an expected part of their normal growth and generative capacity.

In the end, it is the miracle of preaching, the magic of the gospel, that dispels the gloom again from this much-miracled, time-wearied Camelot of ours, and sets its knights and ladies all adance again. Nothing else can out-Merlin it; it is the supreme gift of God to this soul-spent, jag-jaded age we live in. And woe to the man to whom it is put in trust if he be not worthy of trust!

All of this has not been to say that a proper conception of Christian education and its relation to the preaching ministry, or vice versa, will instantly turn any church into a paradise or any minister into a Chrysostom and his people into late-blooming apostolic wonders. There are many levels of intelligence and talent and education in churches. Some respond more readily and agreeably to corrected situations than others; some make correction virtually impossible. But there is no church anywhere, under any condition or set of conditions, that will not realize with a sense of marvel and gratitude a definite improvement from the advancing and encouraging of its educational program along the lines I have tried to suggest.

The feeling of unity and progress, when the pulpit and the teacher's lectern are in benevolent and harmonious relationship, with one challenging and feeding the other, belongs to any people of God. It is their right, their privilege, their legacy. And there is no place where this improved relationship can be better initiated and promoted than in the pulpit itself.

And when the minister, that black-robed crow of the gospel, that stuttering croaker of the Word too dangerous to come in plainer utterance, begins to see the seeds he has sown for the relationship coming back home to the pulpit with plenteous increase, like a sudden field of corn he never remembers planting—when Christian education helps to bring to fruition and perfection what is born in the effort of preaching—he will have his reward.

5

PREACHING AND CHURCH ADMINISTRATION

About church administration I must confess that I am by nature a Jeffersonian: That government is best which governs least, which functions with a few large, overreaching principles and with a minimum of scrutiny and interference on minor matters. There is something self-defeating, if not self-exhausting, about the administrator who, having established lines of authority and patterns of cooperation, is even then unable to relax his superintendence of routinized office work, but labors under the irresistible compulsion to inspect and straighten out the work of his subordinates. To my mind, the real secret of administration lies in the thoughtful selection of colleagues and committeemen who will in turn deal imaginatively and responsibly with their respective duties. The administrator is himself then freed to do what he is presumably best at; that is, he is able to devote his time to reflection upon the overall contours of the organization, to probing critically and helpfully into apparently unhealthy areas of the corporate life, to constructing new approaches to the organizational aims and fresh configurations of power and influence.

This means, applied to the pastorate, that the more creative minister is one who establishes a responsive and reasonably efficient administrative structure, staffed with professional help or parish personnel who will perform acceptably in their respective roles, and then, apart from regular periodic reassessments of the structure and its adequacy in meeting the needs of the church, accepts his comparative freedom as the opportunity to provide for his parish a sensitive, careful ministry of the Word of God. He does not dissipate his valuable energies in stuffing up the chinks of a tumbledown, haphazard ecclesiastical program or in senselessly duplicating the effort of an associate. He does not abdicate his pulpit for the parish administration of paperclips and inactive membership files.

Half the trouble with most poorly organized and inefficient parish ministries resides in the failure of the senior minister to spend an initial day or week, which must be repeated at intervals, clearly defining his organization, its aims and goals, and the duties of subordinate officers in relation to the total program of the church's ministry. Getting this kind of organizational overview is like getting the initial statement of the purpose of a particular sermon before attempting to write it out—a job which John Henry Jowett said is the hardest but most essential part of preaching. Until we have gotten it we will never have any precise idea of what we are about, and hence will dissipate a large measure of power in the sheer confusion of purpose and effort. One pleasant day spent in fruitful, clear-headed thinking over the aims and methods of church organization will conserve weeks of frustration and inefficacy and muddling later on.

Let me illustrate this with the case of a pastor whom I know. He had been at a particular church for twelve years. Though still a young man, he found his energies nearly depleted. He was not making any reasonable impact with his preaching, or, for that matter, with any other aspect of his ministry. He began to feel, and, indeed, people began to suggest to him, that it was time for him to start over somewhere else. A sense of smothering, of desperation, settled on him, and he couldn't shake it. At last, his back to the wall, he had what we may call "the existential vision." He looked squarely into the possibility of ending his ministry; in his mind's eye he just reduced the whole situation to a zero; and then he began to think clearly about what must be done to rebuild his ministry. His frank analysis of the present state of affairs produced the following conclusions:

Item: He had no daily pattern for his work, no order, no system; consequently he labored always under a sense of pressure and a feeling that things were falling apart.

Item: His helpers in the ministry, from the superintendents of certain church departments right on up through the secretaries and an associate minister, were grossly inefficient. Most of them had been in their positions for years, some for much longer than his own ministry at the church. While it was generally conceded that some of them were incapable of holding their own in a competitive job situation, no one had ever had the courage to suggest their getting out and trying it. Because of this the present minister spent much of his time every day checking the work of these persons, correcting their more flagrant mistakes, and suggesting a play-by-play account of what they should be doing next. His own life, therefore, was dribbling out at the seams.

Item: The government of the church, for the most part, was a government by crisis. Very few important matters were ever met in advance. They were simply received when they came and dealt with under the pressure of the moment. For some church members they provided the only excitement ever to be had in the church; these members had a way of showing up at meetings only when some momentous issue was at hand, threatening to swamp someone or another.

Item: The upshot of it all was that the minister had no time left for a reasonably consistent study of the Scriptures, for planned pastoral calling, for reading new books, for relaxation and wholesome family relationships. He was pushed almost beyond human endurance.

Item: Consequently he had given up any hope, and dream, of a rich pulpit ministry, of sermons intellectually stimulating, biblically thorough, and emotionally redemptive. He had become a bore in the pulpit—the most insufferable thing that can happen to any minister. It was evident to anyone who thought it worth analyzing that even he despaired of his preaching, that thirty minutes of it was almost more than he could endure.

It was a devastating analysis. In existentialist parlance, he was out at the edge of the precipice, staring frightfully into the nothingness of it.

Fortunately, he was made of good stuff. He decided to make a comeback. He began by praying, by thanking God for the dreadful vision of what he had become, of what he had allowed his ministry to become, of what the church had consequently become. He resolved to make straight the way that was crooked. And he began, after praying, by doing the very thing he should have done: he took a vacation. Not really a vacation. It was more like a retreat. He took his family to the seashore for a week. At noontime, when the sun was hot, he romped in the surf with the children or lay on the beach by his wife. But in the early mornings when it was cool and the only sounds were the slapping of the waves and the shrill cries of the sea terns, and again in the evenings when even the birds were hushed and the only noise was the sea, he walked along the shore or sat on a rock or an old log washed in from the sea, and thought. *Thought.*

He carried a little notebook and a pencil with him everywhere he went. And his wife would look out the window of the cabin when she got up and see him bent over that little notebook, carefully inscribing something in it. Then it would go back into his pocket, to be produced again later when something else had been crystallized in his mind. At the end of the week he went home. There was a new note—or one not heard for a long time—in his sermon on Sunday morning. Some of his parishioners congratulated each other for having enjoyed the service for a change and said they would have to send the pastor away for a vacation more frequently. But it was not a one-shot affair. He had loaded for a siege. He did not overturn everything at once. He had enough sagacity to spread his reforms over a period of several months. But it was all there in his mind, all there in his little notebook, and in the weeks and months that followed he worked an utter transformation on the organization and administration of his church. Even the resignations of certain personnel were accomplished with amity, some even with enthusiasm, the questionable persons being transferred into duties more commensurate with their talents or less necessary to the functioning of the church. Important new committees were formed and took vital places of service and governance. One unique committee was established, composed of several of the more reflective and articulate members of the church, two or three being professors in a nearby theological seminary, whose task it was regularly to bring their critical faculties to bear on the organization and outreach of the church's life, to assess its evident preoccupations and measure them against the biblical warrants, and to suggest new means of actualizing the gospel in the lives of the membership. The pastor himself, exhilarated and invigorated by the thrust of his new administrative self-understanding, was able to keep this sort of ferment alive for several more years, until he moved to another church field, making a number of imaginative and dynamic innovations in the program and ministry of the church. And, most important of all to him, he discovered and held a necessary unity in his own life, for he now had time to address himself to what is the perennial task of any minister—the inspired and careful preparation of sermons. The pulpit became the symbolic center of his existence, and from it radiated the meaning and enthusiasm which energized all the tangential committees and organizational arms of the church.

Now we have worked long enough at our subject to be able to come at it more directly and ask in a meaningful context what the relationship of preaching to pastoral administration really is. Do preaching and administration really belong together? Can they be done, both adequately, by the same person? Or are they, like oil and water, unmixable? Should the preacher be an administrator only where it is unavoidable—in smaller churches which cannot afford to hire professional administrative talent? Isn't it better to have a business manager who supervises the total program of the church and holds a position in the staff sort of independent from the senior minister, or at least with cooperative status? Such a plan has well recommended itself to the wisdom of many larger churches. There is, in fact, an annual meeting of professional church business managers, at which papers are presented and dialogue sessions held on such topics as might appear germane to the roles of the participants.

There is of course a real danger involved in the preacher's being the chief administrator of the church, and that is that it is so easy to come to regard preaching as merely another function in the multifaceted business of operating the ecclesiastical institution. A minister who has never especially felt the romance of preaching anyway is particularly susceptible to the gentle wooing of the world of affairs which contends that *it* is after all more important than mere words spoken during a sort of unreal service once each Sunday morning. He soon finds it easier to shuffle some papers around on his desk and dash off to this or that committee meeting than to labor regularly on the theological rockpile in order to produce a properly conceived and executed sermon once a week. It is much the same with the average minister as with the professor whom Jacques Barzun described in *Teacher in America*. The only proper thing to do when morning classes are over is to turn himself to some scholarly thing waiting to be read or written; but he lacks inspiration and energy, so he turns over the desk calendar and sees (thank God!) that there is a meeting at which he is due; it is important, he must attend it, and, as Barzun wryly observes, "it counts as work." It is so much easier to be Marthas than to be Marys, to do the objective and tangible things at hand than to work at the more subjective and intractable things.

But I am not of the opinion that the minister should have nothing to do with the business affairs of the church, any more than I am of the opinion that the professors in a university should have nothing to do with the policies governing the maintenance and operation of the university. It is he, on the contrary, who in the end is capable of giving the kind of direction and superintendence which his institution must have. The minister, like the professor, is the true guardian of the ideals of his institution. This may at times lead to his being or seeming idealistic, and it may be generally conceded that idealism to some extent unfits a man for the business world. But the church and the school are not businesses in the same sense in which a tobacco company and an advertising firm are businesses. They have certain business relationships which they must fulfil; but they do not perform their functions in order to show the same kind of profit which the ordinary business seeks to show. In other words, their business is incidental to their existence in a world which ordinarily proceeds by businesslike methods; the conducting of business is to them a secondary matter, not the primary one. This is not to say that they should not conduct their affairs in a businesslike manner; slothfulness is no excuse in either an educational or an ecclesiastical domain. But it is to say that the ideal must get the prime cut and business take the hindmost whenever there is a conflict between the two.

Now the nature of the church is dictated by the thing that forms the church, by what the church has come into existence in response to, and that is the preaching of the Word of God. Perhaps we need not say the preaching of the Word of God, but only the Word of God, for if that Word could somehow get into us without preaching, then we might simply dispense with the matter of the vehicle by which it comes. But we stand in fee to the Apostle who reminds us that men cannot hear the gospel without preachers. However drastically we may be called on to modify preaching, we shall never dispense with it; it will always be the "center of the center" of things.

A church which exists by virtue of its efficiency of organization is not on that account a church, regardless of the size of its membership or its budget. Unless it has been formed by the Word in its bosom, unless it continues to be shaped and agitated by that Word, it is only posing as a church, and succeeds thus in its imposture only because the world itself understands mainly the external signs of the church and not the internal things which really constitute the nature of the church.

Therefore, we are able to assert with confidence the importance of having a proper relationship between preaching and the administration of the church. The church comes into existence because the gospel is preached, and continues to exist for the purpose of serving the act of preaching the Word and working out its unique results in the lives of men. Sound administration of the church is that which actually supports preaching in this work, which helps to implement, even in the structural life of the ecclesiastical organization, the gospel of Jesus Christ. There is no place in the church for routines and practices which are either neutral and amoral or worldly and acquisitive. The pulpit ministry of the church must be carried directly or implicitly into the most insignificant details of the church's life as an organization; else those details suddenly become significant as barometers of the care which the church really exerts over its pastoral charge.

It is of course apparent that I am pushing here. One can hardly expect to see the preaching of the church reflected clearly and unmistakably in the minor business transactions or committee framework of the institution. Not if one does not know what he is looking for. But the reflection should be there and should be discernible when one does know what he is looking for, or when it is pointed out to him that there is a definite relationship involved. Then he should be able to see certain marks which the preaching has made upon the program of the church, in items all the way from business and finance to group dynamics and interpersonal relations. It should be clear that the preaching has had its influence, has made itself felt, in the lesser spheres of the church's life, redeeming them, as far as it is possible, from the dullness and secularity we often attribute to organizational routines and functions.

How this is so may be understood thoroughly only by the minister who feels that it is so and who determines that it shall be so in his own parish administration. But we can at least make some general observations here and hope, like the impressionist, to suggest much more. The following categories are somewhat arbitrary, but generally constitute, together, the major organizational structure of the church.

General Organization: The Selection and Education of Leaders. No task is of greater importance, in structuring the church for its day-to-day life, than that of developing a responsible framework of church administration. This involves the careful arrangement of a network of committees and boards which will be charged with handling the routine business of the church. Much labor and energy are conserved if from the beginning the lines of communication and authority are clearly defined in the mind of the pastor and in the understanding of the committee members themselves, and if there are enough committees strategically placed not only to provide for the natural contingencies of organizational life but to anticipate, to seek out, to run ahead, to act creatively in behalf of the membership. There are few places where the minister can himself show more imagination and sensitivity than in the selection of his subordinates; and the same goes for these subordinates as they choose their own subordinates. The haphazard method of electing officers and committeemen in a church, simply with a view to filling the roster or to using as many members as possible, is a decadent one, and the minister who employs it deserves what he gets. Moreover, the minister cannot merely appoint subordinates and expect them to work together harmoniously and creatively without further preparation. The task of selection fades into the task of education. Here the minister will do well to follow the example of the Master Teacher, who made no attempt at educating the masses, but chose out a dozen men of varied backgrounds and abilities and invited them to walk with him, dine with him, and talk with him on an intimate basis over a period of months. We not only try to choose more of the leaders than we can possibly know well, but we have a habit of picking those who more or less conform to a certain pattern or stereotype in our thinking of what the typical church leader looks like. Consequently there is a monotony in the appearance and behavior of most church boards and organizations.

But in what relation, if any, does preaching stand to all of this? How can it possibly affect the total organizational pattern of the church? Two or three possibilities occur to me. Again I emphasize that these are mere suggestions for further consideration, springboards to further development in the mind of the inventive reader.

First, a very practical consideration: The preacher who is respected as a preacher, who does a thoughtful and sound job in his pulpit every Sunday, will be listened to more eagerly and carefully by the laymen and fellow clergy who constitute his organization force. This is not my own observation, incidentally, but that of a prominent Methodist minister in the state of California, who said that he could even tell the difference in the air of a committee meeting according to how well he had succeeded in the pulpit the preceding Sunday. A good workman is not without honor, even when he enters a committee meeting.

A second and more profound consideration is this: The seriousness with which the preacher addresses himself to the task of preaching the full gospel of Christ invariably carries over to the board members or committeemen of the church. And, vice versa, a lack of seriousness carries over. If a vital doctrinal substratum underlies the message of the church's pulpit—and note the word *vital!*—then it will in a measure color the work and thinking of those who do the church's business. If the minister wrestles earnestly and fairly with social issues, reminding men always that Christ must be found in our brothers, in the beggars at our doors, in the man of another racial or national origin and of another religious persuasion who has been hurt beside the road, then a social consciousness will pervade the deliberations of the committees of the church. If the sermon makes its presentation or proclamation as clearly and intelligibly as it can and yet always makes plain its own humility, its inability to speak of

God as he really is in his mystery, in his partially undisclosed or undiscoverable identity, then boards and committees are more likely to proceed at their jobs with humility and reverence. And if, on the other hand, the minister is derelict in the preparation of himself and his message; if he is himself doctrinally confused and inconsistent; if he fails to see how the gospel of Christ moves out of our neat theological containers and demands at last to authenticate itself in human relations and social contexts; if he enters the pulpit with no sense of reverence for what he is doing, what he represents, for God or the church or the communion of the saints or the sacramental aspects of worship and life; how can we expect better of the variegated committee life of the church, composed as it is of lay people who have not had the privilege of concerted study and practice in sacred things? In Chaucer's words, "If gold rust, what will iron do?" Again, it is the pulpit that is signal in the life and ministry of the church, that determines the course of that life and ministry.

Moreover, the preaching of the church should be constantly challenging the existing order, probing it and weighing it to discover its shortcomings. This should not be done in a personal manner, of course, so that it is continually offending this brother or that, but in the spirit and vigor of Christ. Organization should not be permitted ever to calcify, to harden into forms incapable of modification; it should always remain living, fluid, dynamic. And preaching that is aware, that is serious, that plays over the work and mission of the church like an unwearying spotlight, can help it to do so. This is a primary matter, and the minister can ill afford to neglect it. It is easier, certainly, to carry on one's preaching ministry in one corner of the church and let the business go on in the other corners. Few of us set ourselves happily to being Atlas, with the world poised precariously on our shoulders, and, in a sense, that is just what the minister does when he tries to extend the influence of his pulpit into all the church's life; but in the end it is the only responsible stance a faithful steward can take.

Staff Relationships. This topic is in a manner covered by the one we have just considered, but merits a special word. Next to the total organizational pattern of the church, few items can claim more importance than the creative Christian relationships among members of the paid church staff. And here again the preaching of the Word, properly appreciated by all the persons on the staff, becomes the basis for relationship. If the sensitive proclamation of the gospel and the realization of the Word in men's lives is the paramount concern in the minds of the staff members, then they have a definite rule of thumb for day-to-day interaction: It is the counsel of Luther, previously quoted in regard to worship, "Let everything be done so that the Word prevails."

How does this touchstone work? Suppose we take two of the thorniest problems in church staff relations, that of the relationship of the senior minister to the minister of music and that of his relationship to the associate minister. In both of these instances, the relationship tends to be strained by the natural competitive instincts of the personalities involved. The friction between the senior minister and the musician is mainly confined to the matter of the worship service and the parts they play there; but the friction between the senior minister and his associate has much wider occasion, in the entire, weeklong ministry of the church.

Ordinarily the main disagreement of the preacher and the musician comes over the question of what music should be used in the service. They may indeed have certain personality conflicts, but where the ministry of the church is concerned they usually are at odds, if they are at odds, over the choice of music. Now: Let them set themselves under our rule of thumb, that the Word must prevail. What happens? Suddenly it is no longer a matter of differing tastes and opinions, at least not to the former extent. A third factor, a point of reference, has been introduced: Does the music play its part in the ministry of the Word? Does it prepare men to hear the Word, even proclaim it for them to hear? And does it provide an adequate means for the expression of their response to this mighty Word? The preacher thus has a check on his own complaints, his own musical idiosyncrasies, and an appeal by which to speak disinterestedly about the music of the church to the director of music. Personalities give way, to some extent, to a more objective criterion for the ministry of worship.

A similar thing may happen in the relationship between the senior minister and the associate minister. It often happens that the associate is a younger man than the senior minister. While sometimes lacking the discipline and wisdom of the older man, he may compensate for this in freshness and vigor and personal warmth. If he is well liked, and is not thoughtful of the welfare of the senior minister and the church as a whole, he may well become the "darling" of certain coteries in the church, and, as such, may be championed against the senior minister as a better preacher, a more incisive thinker, a more muscular Christian, a more active visitor, or even a wiser counselor. He may even be taken in by this unintended rivalry, seduced by the praise of men into actually trying to subvert the ministry of the elder man. These are unpleasant possibilities, but they are enfleshed in our midst all the time.

What does the predominance of the Word say to this situation? Herman J. Sweet has suggested the answer in his worthwhile book on *The Multiple Staff in the Local Church*. He says that the older minister will do well to admit to himself, if it be the case, that he has lived under a number of pressures for several years, and that because of those pressures he is probably not so alert and well informed in some things as the younger man. For example, his main reading fare, aside from the Bible and a couple of study books he halfway finished at a summer conference, has been printed sermons and short articles in religious journals; he has simply not managed the time for strenuous excursions into more intellectually demanding things. Why cannot this man, if he is really more interested in the preaching of the Word than in anything else, take the younger minister unto himself as a friend and mentor in the greater ministry of Christ, listening to him, frequently deferring to him, employing him more responsibly in the leadership of the church, and so, in effect, incorporating their ministries for the sake of the gospel? Won't this work, most of the time, if it is done in a spirit of kindness and service? And can't variations of it be worked in most staff relationships?

Finance. Here is an area of the church's life which the minister often feels embarrassed about, as though it were only a necessary evil and not properly a part of the Christian life at all. Few ministers ever show up in university courses in higher finance. With a sense of thankfulness they leave the surveillance of such matters to the businessmen among the laity, and content themselves with comparing this year's budget with last year's on such items as total income, expenditures for missions, gifts to denominational programs, and local salaries. The average minister could learn a lot more about corporation finance, and could bring his preaching to mean much more to this part of the church's ministry.

This is not to say that he should set himself to preach more often on tithing or on charities and benevolences. Such things should probably never occupy the center stage in our preaching, though they are always waiting in the wings to rush out. If we are faithful to declare the gracious benefits of God, then men's hearts will be sensitized toward their brothers and toward the world mission of the local church. The formula is always that of the Apostle Paul in the fifteenth and sixteenth chapters of I Corinthians: he has been talking about the great ultimates, about sin and death and the grave, about crucifixion and resurrection and victory; and then, as though it were the most natural thing to be said in the sequence, he says, "Now concerning the contribution for the saints . . ."; and he goes on with quite specific instructions about how the contribution is to be made. There is no disjunction; it is certainly not a *non sequitur*. It is the most logical movement imaginable. The great issues of the faith, like the coming of Christ, themselves become enfleshed and enacted into the realm of everyday affairs, where the purse of man plays a vital and necessary part.

There is our clue. The true preaching of the gospel always moves quietly, even imperceptibly, from grace to responsibility, from the indicative to the imperative, from benefit to obligation; and therefore it is from first to last involved in the worldly business of church finance.

From first to last, that is, if it also plays the major part in governing the way the money is spent. The preacher's responsibility is not ended when the money has been gathered; he cannot then wash his hands and say, "There you have it, I am innocent from this point on." On the contrary, faithful preaching alone can adequately inform the financial conscience of the church and keep it sensitive and worthy in the discharging of its stewardship.

The Apostle did not let the matter rest when he had exhorted the saints to lay by on the first day of the week: on more than one occasion he became the bearer and the distributor of the funds, accompanying them to their intended destination. In a similar way, no minister has finished his duty when he has inspired Christian people to give their offerings to God; then he must also inspire the distribution. Most people today, unfortunately, do not have an adequate sense of the stewardship of their goods—at least not in America, where a phenomenal amount of wastage indicts us for being less than careful with what we have. And churches are no less guilty. One sometimes feels that so much is spent on organizational overhead and programming, both at the local and denominational levels, that very little of what is provided by the saints actually arrives at a useful destination. It is rather like having a gold pipeline of large dimensions to carry a trickle of water from a spring that is dry anyway part of the year. Preaching cannot be doing its business when it lacks the prophetic conscience to deal with such things; it is concerned with them from beginning to end. Only as it seizes its responsibility in this way does church finance come to reflect the gospel in an intimate and recognizable fashion.

The Church Facing the World. Closely allied to the matter of finance is the subject of the total outreach of the church, of its mission, its program for making the gospel heard in the world at large. There are many avenues for this outreach, both locally and abroad. But basically, strictly speaking, preaching *is* the mission of the church and the mission of the church *is* preaching; and even when they are not thought of as synonymous, it must be recognized that it is preaching that both initiates and sustains the mission enterprise of the church. By making the gospel a lively ferment in the lives of the congregation, preaching keeps the church on course, keeps it oriented toward its mission field. The gospel is not social in its origin, as the humanists would have us believe, but it is indisputably social in its results. It cannot be faithfully and sensibly preached without issuing directly in huge efforts to clear slums, establish settlement houses, integrate races, feed orphans, clothe the poor, rehabilitate the alcoholic and the addict, and generally offer a more humane way of life to men in distress and brokenness.

If the vast galaxy in which our sun is only a very poor star were in the imagination reduced to the size of a football field, then the earth on which we live would probably be invisible to a man standing on the sidelines and looking hard for it. It is to this world, a mere blip of dust caught up momentarily in a surprisingly orderly whirlpool of air, that God came in Christ. And the very shockingness of the distance, the disproportion of it, when carefully proclaimed from the pulpit, should make it easier for any man in the pew to look through the same gospel at a half-naked aborigine squatting by a muddy pool of water in western Australia or some cocoa-skinned child following a rude wooden plow behind a deliberate old ox in the north of India, and to see there not a spectacle but a brother. In other words, preaching helps to establish in an external fashion, separated from itself, what it already is in the world: the mission of God and the church.

Beyond these major areas of the church's organization there are numerous minor ones—the matter of its building, of its publicity, of its recreation, and so on—each of which depends in its own way upon preaching. It is the preaching of the church, for example, which, through the consistency of its theology and the vitality of its proclamation, determines to a greater or lesser extent the architecture and decoration of the local church. Sermons with a flimsy or confused theology will be reflected in a congregation with hazy notions about what their church's architecture should represent or "say," if anything. Amos Wilder speaks in *Theology and Modern Literature* of one church architect who was surprised to learn that the congregation which had retained him had no clear idea at all of what their new building should express; they simply wanted a church, and could not understand that he should question them about their beliefs before drawing up the plans. But where the preaching is strong and of an inner consistency, men begin to straighten their own muddled thinking about such things, and to be concerned for the proper symbolism, in order that the architecture of the church be both functional and accurate in its visual representation to the world of what is preached in that church.

The same is true of publicity. The advertising policies of the church, all the way from the bulletin board or the sign in front of the building to the Saturday notice in the town paper or the poster inviting attention to a special meeting, are influenced in large measure by the tone and content of what is preached from the pulpit. What can be our judgment of the pastor of George Babbitt's church in Sinclair Lewis' novel *Babbitt*, when Babbitt conceived the idea of hiring a hot newspaper man to ballyhoo the Sunday school, putting gossipy notices in the paper about goings-on in the school and headlining the lessons in a sensational way, as, for example, in a lesson on Jacob and Esau, "Jake Fools the Old Man, Makes Getaway with Girl and Bankroll"? Our judgment in this case should be kind, to be sure, for Babbitt could not honestly be said to have spent much time in the pew. But the offense against propriety is little short of what we witness every day on the part of some church where the gospel is distorted by a bizarre presentation. The best preaching, on the other hand, creates an aura in a church that deters, if it does not stop, such inappropriate gestures of publicity. In sensitizing men to the spirit of Christ, it develops an inner caution against neon lights and phosphorescent colors and cheap paper banners, against anything that smacks of the bistro or the circus or the county picnic.

I mentioned recreation because that may seem so totally unrelated to preaching and theology and biblical study as not to belong in this discussion. But I wonder if that is so. George Buttrick once answered a man who was evidently bristling about a certain church's spending money on a gymnasium by telling him about one of the recreational leaders in his own congregation when he was pastor of Madison Avenue Presbyterian Church in New York. The leader had been substituting players freely in a basketball tournament, and one of the boys, fearing they would lose the game that way, complained. The next day the leader set a ladder up under the goal and made that boy sit on top of it and drop the ball through the goal five hundred times. "That's what you really care about," he said. It was not necessarily the preaching that prepared the way for the leader's attitude, but I would dare to suggest that the preaching helped, especially in that church.

In short, there is very little, if anything, in the organization and administration of the local church that may not be touched and turned in toward center by vital, nourishing preaching. It should be a matter of real joy to us to extend our pulpit ministries into as many areas as possible, not being content to have dropped a bomb on the territory, but wishing also to be the mop-up troops, moving in to assure the most effective use of the bombing. For only our preaching is able to provide the lodestone for the drawing together of all our ministries; only the pulpit is able to become the focus, the means of integration, in an institution which has already come, in many places, to mean big business.

Just as the church in the days of its infancy borrowed pagan rhetoric for its preaching forms and pagan architecture for its places of worship, and just as it has always appropriated easily from things cultural or philosophical those which would fit usefully into the Christian order, so we may today profitably adopt the knowledgability and methods of modern business, keying them to the service of the church of the Lord Jesus Christ. But by the same analogy we are under obligation to transmute what we borrow, to invest it with our own principles and ethical convictions, to baptize it, as it were, into the highest and purest usage to which it may be put: that of helping to realize, as much as such things can, the coming of the Kingdom of God.

6

THE CENTRALITY OF PREACHING IN THE PERSON AND LIFE OF THE MINISTER

Real preaching, as the poetic thin line between the mystery and the plainness of the world we live in, is always a vital part of the continuum of Christian history. As Gustaf Wingren says in *The Living Word,* what happens in the pulpit is itself "a part of that series of acts which the Bible depicts and which ends in the resurrection of the dead."

Unfortunately, we lose sight of this truth all too easily. The world of the Bible seems hopelessly far in the past, a million light-years from where we are today. Many are saying that the continuum of Christian history has reached the end of its track in our time and has crashed through the barriers and run aground in an open field where it is disconcertingly peculiar and out of place. Ours is the extremest sense of contemporaneity any age has ever had. It is almost as if we were separated by some major surgery from all the institutions and beliefs of the past.

The minister especially has suffered from this phenomenon of disjunctiveness. Megalopolis, technocracy, nuclear fission, interplanetary probes, have all conspired to date him, to relegate him

to the past, to make him the most singular anachronism on the
professional scene. Shifting nervously from one foot to the other
under the sombre robes of his uneasy office, he seems more a
ghost from the past than an inhabitant of the present. He reminds men more of candlelight processions and chilly cathedrals
and wheezy old organs than of anything in the modern world of
nylon and plastic, and they put a coin in his hand for the sake
of their nostalgia and the days of long ago.

Many ministers have consequently become quite busy about
little things—memoranda, antependia, the cut of their pulpit
gowns. They are determined to be faithful in the management of
small things in the hope that someday, perhaps in a fairer world,
they will be graduated again into the management of the larger.
They fuss with the printers about the design of the typeface on
the insert for the bulletin, haggle with the choirmaster over the
fivefold amen which he prefers to the sevenfold, dispute with
the building and grounds committee about the particular shade
of celestial blue to be used in repainting the sanctuary, lecture
the affianced on the inviolability of certain traditions affixed to
the marriage ceremonies and preparations therefor, and generally
make nuisances of themselves to their families and anybody else
who has sustained contact with them. They are determined, since
the invalidation of their credentials, to demonstrate the inde-
fatigability and scrupulosity of their officialdom and petty bu-
reaucracy. It alone having been left to them, they are bent with
fury upon its eternal and everlasting preservation!

There is no cynic, I have discovered, who is worse than a
clerical cynic, worse than a minister who has become unsure of
his faith and his calling, who has lapsed into the situation I have
just been describing. There is no talking to such a man. He
knows all the vocabulary, all the arguments, all the answers; he
has been over them a thousand times in his own mind.

I remember being with a dear friend one evening when he
was going through a period of great despair in his career as a
clergyman. We were sitting at the end of the pier on a little lake
in the piney-wood country of southern Georgia, casting our lines

and pulling in an occasional flip-flopping little fish as the sun disappeared, dust-red and then dark, over the far treetops. It was one of the quietest, most beautiful evenings I can recall having had in many years. We didn't say much. We just sat there. What was there to say? He knew his theology as well as I, and was more experienced in the pastorate. I'm sure he could recite more of the Scriptures, for he is gifted with a wonderful memory. There wasn't anything I could tell him, any remonstration I could make, that he hadn't rehearsed again and again in his own mind. It was just a time for sitting and fishing, for watching the sun go down and the moon come up, for hearing the far-off splash of a fish or the croak of a frog or the cry of a loon.

The truth was, as he and I both knew, that his feeling of malaise was not something that could be patched up by talking at all. It was much deeper than that. It had something to do with the nature of his experience. He had lost the *why* out of the middle of life, out of the middle of what he was doing, and the why is never easy to put back. Therefore all of life had become dull and metallic tasting to him. What was left to a man who had lost sight of the only goals he had ever known?

What does a man do when it happens to him? What do you and I do—for it happens also to us? If we are able to do anything, if our resources are deep and at least partially self-generative for a while, we probably do what my friend did—we wait. We go fishing. We take a vacation. We go to Europe. We give the restorative processes a chance to do their work. We know that our lives are always more than the sum of our present thoughts and feelings, that these may indeed grossly misrepresent who we really are and how we really feel down below the waterline of our conscious minds, down where worlds are made and unmade all the time. So we wait and watch, watch and wait, in hope that what once tenanted our beings and made them alive with daily joy and expectancy will one day come back and resume tenancy again.

We may regard it as a time of growth, of expansion and acquisition, when life seems overtaxed because it is going through the diastole movement of the systole-diastole rhythm, when it is expelling stale old thoughts and dependencies in order to restore the self with new ones with new nerve and new insight and new direction. We may take courage from remembering what the mystics have often called "the dark night of the soul," and know that that is what is occurring with us, that it is dark now but will be light again, will be luminous with the brightness that only the dark can induce. We may therefore seize the occasion for invading new territory in the world of thought, for dreaming in new philosophies, reading in new writers, dabbling in new forms of self-expression (even when we are unsure of the self we try to express). And when faith comes back, when belief and hope and joy return, it will be in new vestments, *au courant* and meaningful to our ministries. We may even wonder how we could live and minister without such periods, or without the growth and understanding they seem to occasion.

What really lies at the root of cynicism in a minister? Sometimes it is unpleasant experiences, either in his own life or with the people he is in constant contact with. But far more commonly it is not the direct result of anything in particular, but is the product of a slow and steady attrition. It grows in the absence of a vital, active faith. It occurs when a minister loses sight of his *raison d'être*, when he loses his vision of what the ministry is all about, of what he is contending for, and permits his daily work to degenerate into a dispiriting series of errands and small jobs, both at church and afield.

And this is terrifying, for which of us doesn't fall into that dangerous situation at times? We don't intend for it to happen to us, of course, but the trouble is that it happens before we know it, and then we are caught!

I remember a particularly vivid dream I had one night during a bad period in my own life. The main feature of the dream was some kind of treasure hunt, though the treasure itself was never defined and its location never became certain (both of which facts intensified a Kafkaesque sense of confusion and of incredible scurrying and maneuvering to discover the hiding place). I was riding in one of those hopeless little cars that clowns drive in circuses and at country fairs—the kind that are infernal contraptions, going now forwards and now backwards, now jolting to a halt and rearing up on the back wheels, now whirling around in a full circle, now coughing and sputtering or erupting in vile clouds of smoke, or belching and exploding in a final sort of catastrophe. It was, at best, a very uncertain ride. You can imagine my anxieties, trying to arrive in haste at a treasure whose whereabouts were completely unknown, and yet riding in a dilapidated and treacherous vehicle whose ways were wholly unpredictable and unmanageable. Activity was maximal and progress was worse than minimal!

All kinds of simple, everyday tasks were involved in the search, which, like any treasure hunt, required the completion of certain ridiculous assignments before the next clue or stage of the hunt could be disclosed. One of the tasks, I remember, had to do with taking a bundle of white shirts to a laundry and then returning at a later time to retrieve them. I recall that the pressure in the race (for I seemed to be competing with other contenders for the prize, though they remained unknown to me) had built to a climax at the moment when I received from the laundry clerk the ticket on my shirts. I returned to the wicked little car and sat in it, rotating and bucking, while I tried to decipher a coded message on the ticket. At last, in a moment of illumination, the meaning of one part of the code flashed clearly and precisely into my mind. I shall spare you the obscenity, but it was a two word Anglo-Saxonism commonly found in public restrooms and meaning, "Perform an erotic act on yourself!"

There was a criticism of my life that I could not possibly ignore! Apparently that was the punchline of the entire dream, for I then awoke into a state of semi-consciousness, and, to my knowledge, had no more dreams that night. But what a dream! And what a punchline! I had to admit, as I stood at the breakfast counter the next morning and sawed around the edge of half a grapefruit, that it was an effective word for the sterile and unproductive busy work I had been so completely absorbed in in recent weeks.

What I needed, I now realized, was to escape from the tyranny of a hundred inconsequential little things by recentering my life and thought on the great pivotal truths of the gospel. I needed a more positive grasp of the matter of our faith and the message of our preaching. Lacking such a grasp, my subconscious had broken through in a dream to sound the alarm and launch an attack on the problem.

It is bad enough that a man will let his life get in a shape like this, but what happens to his preaching when it does? Must it not inevitably become thin and brittle, or else hollow and empty? Must it not betray to those who listen that it does not really know the peace of which it speaks or the resources of which it prattles, that it is in fact a dubious exercise concocted by a man who knows he must have something to say in public or else come to forego the monthly check from the church that sustains him and his family? Must not such preaching eventually defame the pulpit and dishonor the church and disparage the congregation? And must it not taste bitter and dry in the mouth of the one speaking it?

Here is what one layman wrote about his minister, a man who often managed to preach very good sermons though he was personally depleted of faith and inclined to be caustic and little in his personal relationships: "There is one problem I cannot resolve. How does one manage to ignore the character of the man who gives expression to spiritual thoughts in the pulpit? I know that the best of ministers are human beings prone to all the temptations which assault all men. . . . But my need is for a man I can admire and want to imitate, a man whose goodness, patience, brotherly love, and active and applied Christianity make me want to be like him. As it is, I feel that my going to church, instead of helping me to live a better life, is week by week, drop by drop, turning me sour at what to me (rightly or wrongly) seems like blatant hypocrisy."

What has happened to a minister like that? How has he permitted his existence to get so far out of hand? How does he manage to go on in the role of minister from day to day and week to week?

Helmut Thielicke has suggested in his book *The Trouble with the Church* that it is the sort of thing that can happen to any man who forgets that faith begins to dwindle whenever it is denied entrance to any part of his daily existence. Thielicke was visiting a church councilman who lived in the remains of a lovely home that had been bombed during the war. He expressed his regret to the host that the bombs had done so much damage, but the host brushed it aside. "Even in this loss," the man said, "I experienced the grace of God." Thielicke was ashamed for having ventured his sentiment; here indeed was a noble Christian soul. But then the host continued: "God left me with just enough room so that I did not have to take in any refugees after the war." At a stroke the man had destroyed every opinion of his nobility. He was apparently a devout person, but, said Thielicke, he seemed never to have suspected that his faith or his relationship to God made any special demands of him during the time of the housing shortage. This was an area of his life that was sealed off against what he professed to believe about Christian commitment; faith simply had no relevance for it.

I suspect that this was the trouble with the minister whose parishioner expressed so little confidence in him. And isn't it the same with all of us? Aren't there times when our lives become so fragmented and compartmentalized that we fail to feel deeply and convincingly the relationship between them and the gospel we somehow go on preaching?

Maybe it would be better to have a smaller gospel, one less adequate and exciting than ours, and for it to extend its domain completely throughout our lives, than to have such an enormous gospel that we despair of its ever being relevant to our daily existence. But we can put it quite bluntly: if the gospel does not wash with us it will not wash with those who hear us. We are too transparent, too open, too readable, for that. If the light at the core of our lives is not the *lux Christi,* the light of Christ,

then our congregations will discern it and will not really hear—
not with the inner ear, where hearing is transmuted into life
and action.

Let us put it quite plainly: the rhythm and reciprocity between a man's preaching and his other pastoral functions, of
which we have spoken, is rarely if ever more important than in
this matter, in the relationship of a man's preaching and his
personal life as a minister. The gospel which is announced in
our preaching must be reified, must take actual form and substance, in our daily affairs; and, when it is, our daily affairs will
begin to be seen, both by us and by others, in a role supportive
to our preaching. This is *the* essential harmony for the minister;
there is no other quite so important as it. If he has it, then both
his life and his work, his private affairs and his public duties,
will continue to provide him with stimulus and joy. He will not
be bothered by "poor circulation of faith," and his people will
not complain of incredible speeches.

Consider, for example, the crucial relationship between a minister and his family. If a man does not have an understanding
of how his professional and private existences are related, how
they come together, he will be constantly torn in the tension
between them, and may even eventually come to prefer one to
the other.

The question of time is primary. What minister's wife does
not complain occasionally, at least in the intimacy of the home,
of her unwilling sacrifice of a husband not only to a strenuous
calling but also to the apparently illimitable demands of the
particular congregation he serves? What minister's child does
not turn from answering the phone, a hand over the receiver,
and announce disdainfully, "Oh, daddy, it's *that* woman again"?
This is natural. The minister is the servant of many people. The
family cannot help wondering why they don't get at least equal
time with all the others.

One minister's son I heard of was quite enterprising. His
father had been promising to spend an afternoon playing ball
with him, but one thing after another had intervened to frus-

trate their intentions. Finally the boy appeared at his father's office one day and asked if he might have an appointment. Asked why he wanted one, he replied, "You always keep your appointments."

No man wants to fail these other human beings whom he loves so inexpressibly. Whenever he leaves the dinner table and goes to his study to work at a sermon or read a new book, it is always with a feeling of guilt and reluctance. But the work must be done. Certainly it will not do itself.

How does the minister square his professional life with his private one? How does he work out a *modus vivendi,* a way of getting on, that will be fair to both of these important areas of his existence?

Suppose we ask whether he really believes what he preaches on Sunday morning. Is his world view the one he espouses in the pulpit? Is there something definitive about God's having revealed himself in Jesus Christ? Do we really live in last days, in the time before the end of time? Is the whole mad welter of human life and human pain to be resolved finally along the lines of the Sunday gospel? If the answer is yes, then there is something here capable of polarizing the disparate experiences and responsibilities of this man's calling. There is a formula for resolving questions of conflicting interest.

The formula is this: There is nothing in any man's life that is demeaned or devalued by having to take second place to the publicizing of such a gospel. There is nothing worthy that will not find even higher and finer expression when cast in a role supportive to this task. There is no relationship between a man and a woman that cannot be enhanced and ennobled by its being understood in the light of his calling to preach the gospel, and there is no rapport between a father and his children that cannot be strengthened and sensitized by their mutual acknowledgment of this prior claim upon him and, indeed, upon all of them.

This is not to say that it is always a simple task to say what the best interests of the gospel are. Not even a Solomon could decide with infallibility every time that *this* committee meeting is important and *this* hospital call is necessary and *this* bit of paperwork is worthwhile and *this* civic appearance is urgent. There are times when going out to dinner with his wife or to a ball game with the children is probably far more important to one's gospel, in the long run, than most of the other tasks waiting to be performed. But if a man is fair-minded, if he is willing to admit this and live by it, then his family will realize that he does not ever shut them out arbitrarily, that he does not willfully sacrifice them out of blindness or professional obsession, that he does attempt to weigh the issues and make responsible decisions about his work as a minister and his life as a father and husband.

Time magazine once carried a long article about Bill Moyers, the Long Island newspaper publisher who was at that time special assistant to President Lyndon B. Johnson. Moyers, a young man with a growing family, held a post that made almost superhuman demands upon his time and energy. The *Time* reporter asked him how his family felt about this. He replied that it was true that he was usually under pressure. Several times in recent weeks he had had to cancel the family's plans for a picnic in the country. But it was always explained to the children that their father was needed by the President, and their disappointment was overweighed by a sense of patriotism and pride that their father was serving the nation. They felt that they were making their own contribution in this manner to the needs of the government.

Is the analogy too strained? Let the father be a minister, a man called by God and ordained by the church to preach news of victory and then to pursue it into the lives and personal needs of those who hear. Now what is the situation? Of course the husband and father does not want to neglect his family. He hates to leave his wife to her knitting for another evening and wishes he didn't have to miss the ball game with the youngsters. But they are part of the team too. They help make his ministry work. Their mature acceptance of his role, their encouragement, their assurance of love and support, are essential parts of his day-to-day life. The minister's calling is a high one, but so is that of his family. And the rewards which he reaps are in a very real sense theirs also. When they give him up for a higher purpose, they are sharing in that purpose themselves.

It is imperative, as I suggested before, that the minister not carry this principle to the point of abuse. Most of us have known clergymen who have made of their callings pious excuses for all but abandoning their families. It is so easy for a man who has failed at his work for reasons entirely owing to his own nature to blame those closest to him for the failure.

The truth is that the polarizing work of what we preach ought to affect us and the value-judgments we make as much as it affects those who are involved with us in our calling. It ought to help us to audit and evaluate everything we do. It ought to enable us to separate really significant things from all the trivialities and bring genuine order to our undertakings. It ought to aid us in drawing the lines beyond which the best interests of our calling do not demand that we go, and beyond which they are not truly served.

It is impossible to overemphasize how essential this is to the maintenance of the minister's freedom as a person and an individual in his own right. As Paul Tournier said in an essay on *Fatigue and Modern Society,* it is important that a man determine which things he does not need to do and ought not to do as well as those things he ought to do. Otherwise his life is spilled out at the seams, is squandered and wasted for nothing.

A friend of mine told me about visiting a prominent clergyman a few years ago. While he and the clergyman were talking in the clergyman's office, the telephone buzzed and the secretary said that a certain woman wished to speak to the minister. "Tell her I'm not in," said the minister. A few minutes later there was another buzz and another request from the same woman. "Tell her I'm still not in," said the minister. "She says to leave a note for you," said the secretary, "and to have you call her immediately upon your return." "Then tell her I won't be in," said the minister; "tell her I'm out of town and won't get back until late tonight." A few moments later, the secretary was back on the line: "She says to leave the note anyway and to tell you to call her regardless of what time it is." "Then tell her," said the exasperated clergyman, "to go to hell!"

This outburst of humanness both shocked and delighted my friend. I do not know any further particulars of the story, as I think my friend did not, but I suspect that the woman and her problems were well known to the clergyman—perhaps too well known. She may have been one of those persons, to be found in every parish, who think of the minister as a kind of professional bellboy whose mission it is to answer everybody's call for an aspirin or an apéritif, whatever the hour and whatever else he happens to be doing.

But there are appropriate boundaries between the demands of parishioners and the personal life of the minister, boundaries which may be discerned by asking how relevant the demands are to the preaching and enacting of the gospel. The gospel thus protects the minister at the same time that it exposes him; it does not cast him into the public arena to be taken advantage of by every crank and cannibal in the community.

Again it is true, though, that the monitoring of our work is not merely a defensive matter. Most of us need more protection from ourselves than we do from our parishioners. Fatigue and nervous exhaustion are becoming more and more prevalent among ministers, and frequently they are the fault of men who simply cannot stop going, who secretly fear that if they do they will collapse or disintegrate. We are like all the other professional men in an age when business has become the engrossing fact of life. We can't keep our office work out of the home because we don't want to keep it out, because we can't lock it up at five o'clock and walk away from it, because we have got to be neurotically picking at it and worrying over it wherever we are and whatever we're doing.

"It's gotten so bad with me," wrote one corporation man, "that I have had to make myself stop working at home evenings. I can't read the shortest report without my mind going into action to plan what to do next. I've found this stimulated my mind so much that I couldn't go to sleep at a reasonable hour. What I really wish is that there were more hours in the business day."[1]

Isn't it the same with the minister? The more complex his parish becomes, the more persons he is responsible for, the larger the budget he must supervise, the more involved his staff relationships are, the more inclined he is to blur the boundaries between his working life and his private life so that he transgresses against the latter in his ambition to satisfy the former. Even if he can manage in the evening to get beyond earshot of the telephone, which in the average parish house rings almost incessantly, he still tends to be preoccupied with his work and to mull over and over in his mind the problems and issues which face him as a pastor and administrator.

We are trying to be realistic. Perhaps the minister's similarity to men in other professions will give us a handle on this problem of relating the domestic and professional sides of his existence. What is the best relationship for a man in another profession— say the foreman of a steel mill or the president of a pharmaceutical company? Can he build an impenetrable wall between his eight-to-five existence and his home life? Sociologists do speak today of the commuter's curtain and the effect of distance between home and business as a means of separating the two areas of life. But it hardly strikes us as healthy for a man to live two entirely distinct lives. Whatever tensions or problems he may have, they are only intensified by his attempt to become a doublet of himself, so that there are really two persons and not one living in his skin—one in evidence when he is with his family and the other when he is at his place of business.

It would seem much better for there to be a reasonable amount of communication between the man and his family about what his work is like, how it is going, what he is excited about or bothered about, and, generally, what he does with his time and energy when he is away from home. And the family, conversely, should discuss its interests with the husband and father. If a man and woman are really to be one flesh, then such communication

---

[1] *The Executive Life,* by the Editors of *Fortune* (New York: Doubleday and Co., 1956), p. 70.

is essential. When I try to imagine a healthy picture of a business executive's home life, it is one in which the wife and children not only possess enough information for making relatively accurate assessments of the husband-father's work and working relationships, but actually enter with some enthusiasm into his hopes and disappointments in the business world, so that he catches the 8:15 in the morning with the good feeling down inside that his family is behind him all the way, supporting him with interest and ambition and love for the things he must do that day, whether they are really exciting and creative or merely routine and unimaginative. The man in this kind of situation is a whole man. He is not a Dr. Jekyll and Mr. Hyde, leading one life at home and another at the office. He feels a sense of completeness and unity about his existence, and knows, regardless of how competitive or demanding his job may become, that life is somehow basically good and rewarding for him. And on the other hand, when there are bad times at home, as there are bound to be, the fact that he has not despised his work because of his home, or felt guilty about it because it took him away from his family, allows his pleasure in his work to take the supportive role for a while and carry him along until things are better at home again.

Isn't such a relationship plainly commendable to the clergyman as well? Why shouldn't he turn to his family with the burdens and pleasures of his office, too, and so distribute them as to make them his family's as well as his own? How else can they be a real unit as a family? He will of course not try to tell them every detail, smothering them in trivialities that have not greatly affected him; and there are instances in which he will choose to shield them from unnecessary exposure to misery or misunderstanding as he has encountered them. But there should be between man and wife and father and children a rapport which insists by its very nature upon an easy kind of communication among them—a natural flow of information and affection and sympathy and encouragement, so that they feel themselves to be a single *nephesh,* as the Hebrews put it, a single soul, with each member of the family being a genuine extension of the whole.

Most of us have not taken seriously enough our responsibility to educate our wives and children in our vocation, to share with them and engage with them in meaningful dialogue about the nature and obligations of our work. What wife is so insensitive that she will not rise in some measure to the challenge of the Christian ministry when she sees it as her husband does? Or what child is so autistic that he will not respond to the real meaning of the gospel as it is explained to him and as he begins to see its relevance to him and his freedom and his family relationships—including his father's professional life?

Engaging with others in dialogue is, as I have said before, a risky business. It means laying our own prejudices and understandings out alongside of the other person's so that as we reason together there is danger of ours and his getting all mixed up, and that we will go away thinking as he thought. Dare we do this as ministers? Dare we expose ourselves so completely, gambling the roles we have adopted and the images by which we conceive of ourselves and our ministries? We must, if we are to have integrity in our families and if we are to speak credibly when we speak of the gospel.

Such a practice may seem frightening at first. But in the end it means a sounder and more authentic ministry, and one in which we may rejoice all of our lives, for it goes a long way toward resolving those unnecessary tensions between the minister and his family, the feelings of the family that they aren't included, and the feeling of the minister that he must do his work in spite of his family, as though they were some kind of burden he had to bear while trying juggler-like to keep all the balls in the air. And if the gospel is indeed a gospel for the human situation, a gospel for the man or woman in the disturbed family relationship, then will not any preacher's message be stronger and more convincing if he has himself witnessed the workings of that gospel in his own household and in the personalities of his own loved ones? When he stands to declare divine truth, will he not do so with a more mature grasp of its real incarnation, of the dispersal into the human situation without which it is only so much cultic hocus-pocus, of its wish and need to find particular occasion in the heartaches and soul cries of the people who hear it?

Thus does the message to be preached, indeed the very preaching of it itself, become the focal point of our lives as ministers, the thing eliciting hope and unity in the jumbled affairs of our entire existence, because somehow, in the attempt to make a sound witness to the gospel we have seen and heard, we are forced to discover whether we have in fact really seen it and heard it and to test its reliability in our own experience. Whatever we find out about ourselves and the gospel, the very process gives the gospel another chance to work on us. And we turn from this fresh working of the gospel to declare it again in the pulpit —without oldness, without weariness, without staleness. The Word is always renewing itself in this manner. And the man who preaches is always being renewed by virtue of the fact of his handling it.

I remember how fearfully I began my own ministry. I conceived of the gospel as a very narrow set of facts which one got by memory and then believed in—or tried to believe in. Preaching was almost always a strain, because it seemed to have for its chief business the judging of life—mainly in a negative sense— by that set of facts. And life itself was a strain, because it always seemed so far away from what I was trying to preach. The two didn't seem to belong together at all. The longer I preached the more I felt like a man standing with one foot on the shore and the other on a boat that was slowly pulling out to sea. And the upshot of it was that I wasn't a real person at all, but a minister trying to be a minister trying to be a minister trying to be a minister. I was very unhappy. My life was tedious and artificial, and the excitement which I had once felt for the gospel had turned into the hideous routine of being a parson and having to preach sermons.

My wife, who was quite young when we married, was generally very tolerant of my efforts at right belief and right practice, and, though I am certain she was inwardly disturbed by the prospect of being wed for a lifetime to such a strong-headed man, acceded to my legalistic definitions of the so-called Christian home. Together we worked at the business of being a proper minister and minister's wife.

I do not know when the change in us occurred, or to what it is to be attributed, but something did happen to us. Somewhere along the way we began to understand that the real gospel does not come to us in prepackaged forms, ready for instant and easy consumption. It comes instead disguised as part of our natural existence, as part of what we are as human beings. It has something to do with finding out who we are, quite apart from any creed or credentials, and *becoming* who we are.

My wife and I didn't know who we were. We were all mixed up. And our religious tradition didn't help matters. If anything, it only added to the confusion. We felt as if we were lost in a hall of mirrors, where nothing was what it seemed to be. Slowly, deliberately, we had to try to pick our way along to an exit. We had to find the open air again.

I don't mean to imply that we know all the answers now. We don't. But the experiences we have had along the way have been great ones. For one thing, we found that in trying to rediscover ourselves we really rediscovered each other all over again. Our life together took on variety and wonder. And for another thing, we really began to discover other people. We found that our lives demanded the lives of others for their fulfilment.

I began to see that preaching is an opportunity for getting related to the persons in the congregation. Before, I had had a vague notion that the preacher stands over against the congregation, exhorting it and judging it. But now I realized that preaching exists for the congregation, not the congregation for the preaching. It must reflect the life of the congregation—the real life, the whole life—as much as it does the insights of the Bible or the arguments of theology. The persons of the congregation must recognize something of themselves in it, must feel that it is basically human, even secular. They must realize that they are addressed not by an angel or a mouthpiece or a sermon-machine, but by a man, a man for whom the gospel is as real as biscuits and hominy grits. And, in the encounter of persons, something happens. Life's boundaries are enlarged. Dark places are made light. Hearts are lifted.

People begin to respond to preaching when they can identify with it. They don't just talk about it and accept it as something apart from their existence. They see themselves in it, they take it for the very mirror of who they are, and they want to see the minister to talk more in private about what it means. It affects them deeply.

And when people are affected by our preaching, we are affected in return. Our beliefs metamorphose in the light of what transpires between us and the congregation. We understand ourselves better in terms of our relationships. The same is true with our wives and children. They arrive at new understandings of themselves. It is all dynamic. Life is fluid, ever-changing, exciting. Every new sermon initiates another phase in the ongoing process of our lives together. There is nothing dull or static about any of it.

It is not easy, of course. As Harry Emerson Fosdick once put it, you drench the congregation in your life's blood every time you preach.

But the rewards are inestimable. There is nothing else in life quite so stimulating and full of possibility. Imagine being involved in the moment of another man's discovery of the meaning of life, and of his embarkation on a lifetime's journey of self-development. Doesn't it give you zest for life, and provide meaning for you as well as for him? Just think. It happens all the time when you preach!